QUIET MOMENTS
for TEACHERS

Quiet Moments
for Teachers

Linda McNatt Page

VB
VINE
BOOKS

SERVANT PUBLICATIONS
ANN ARBOR, MICHIGAN

Vine Books is an imprint of Servant Publications especially designed to serve evangelical Christians.

Published by Servant Publications
P.O. Box 8617
Ann Arbor, Michigan 48107

Cover design: PAZ Design Group, Salem, OR

00 01 10 9 8 7

Printed in the United States of America
ISBN 1-56955-063-8

LIBRARY OF CONGRESS CATALOGING-IN-PUBLICATION DATA

Page, Linda McNatt, 1953–
Quiet moments for teachers / Linda McNatt Page.
     p.   cm.
ISBN 1-56955-063-8 (acid free paper)
1. Teachers—Prayer-books and devotions—English.   I. Title.
BV4596.T43P34   1998
242'.68—dc21   98-17019
                                                                                CIP

To my mom,

Martha Ann Abbott McNatt

ACKNOWLEDGMENTS

No book is written by the hand of the author alone. This one is no exception. I would like to thank some of the people whose hearts and hands have touched the pages of my work. My thanks to:

My parents, Lynn and Martha McNatt: Thanks for the deep gene pool and for being my example.

My husband David and my sons, Jeff and Michael: You ate much more fast food than was good for you during this project. Thanks for taking care of baseball games, golf matches, laundry, and even moving to a new home as I worked.

To the women of Friday morning and Monday afternoon Bible study: Your prayers and encouragement kept me going when school and home responsibilities overwhelmed me. Many of your stories appear within. As my way of saying thanks, I have used your names and the names of your children for many of the characters in this book.

To Dr. Kathy Koch: Without your constant and convincing encouragement, this book would never have happened.

To Cindy Tobias: Thank you for introducing my work to Servant Publications.

To Bekah Mulvaney: How can I thank you, my friend, for the hours you spent making sure this project was done well? Thanks for a thousand glasses of iced tea, for the use of your quiet home, and for listening, reading, editing, encouraging, and hyphenating beyond the call of duty. I plan to return the favor someday.

AUTHOR'S NOTE: This work is derived from my twenty-plus years of teaching experience in public schools. Many of the names, descriptions, and circumstances have been changed or combined. Many have not, and where permission was necessary it was obtained. This is a book about reality. If as you read you recognize yourself or your students, then I have succeeded in completing a work that has meaning and value. To God be the glory.

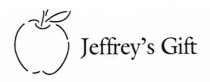 Jeffrey's Gift

A good name is more desirable than great riches.

PROVERBS 22:1

The phone rang at 6:00 on a Sunday morning. All I heard my husband say to my principal on the other end was, "Thank you, Mr. Pearson." I knew in my spirit the news I was about to hear. One of my students, eight-year-old Jeffrey, had died.

Jeffrey had been ill for only about two weeks. His symptoms were those of a simple virus—low-grade fever, headache, sore throat. No one was very worried, until the headache just would not go away. Jeffrey died in an ambulance on the way to a children's hospital in Memphis. The aneurysm that took his life was undetectable until it was too late.

I know I have a soft spot in my heart for children with Down Syndrome, but this little one was especially special. Jeffrey came to our school when mainstreaming was just beginning. Until that year, children with any handicapping condition had been placed in a self-contained classroom. But Jeffrey and the eight other students I taught joined a classroom of students of their own age for lunch, recess, art, music, and library. They were "mainstreaming pioneers," and Jeffrey took to pioneering quite well. He loved the other children and they loved him. The laughter and smiles he brought could not be counted.

Jeffrey and I had a Monday morning ritual. I would ask him what he had done over the weekend. He would lean back in his chair, cross his legs, look up at the ceiling, and say out of one side of his mouth, "S-s-smoke cigars." He would wait for me to tell him it was bad for his health and then throw his head back in laughter. His silver-toothed smile always gave my week the jump-start it needed.

That early morning phone call changed my life forever. I remember standing by Jeffrey's casket thinking that this little one, who was just learning to read and write, now knew the answers to questions that had plagued the minds of philosophers and theologians for centuries. He was in the presence of the Creator who possesses all knowledge. If he could have come back, he would now be the teacher and I the student. He was, in fact, teaching me at that very moment. I learned from him how precious is our time with students, and that I have wasted my day if a student leaves my room with a head full of facts and an empty heart. I learned to capture irreplaceable moments. I learned that I would never cease to learn from those I have been given to teach. I think perhaps that was the day I became a *real* teacher, with the credentials of a broken heart and a passionate spirit.

I made Jeffrey a promise: that if I ever had a son, Jeffrey's name would be carried on. In 1982 I was able to fulfill that promise. May I never forget the one to whom it was made. May I never forget the things he taught me.

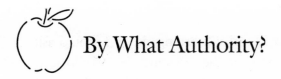 # By What Authority?

"By what authority are you doing these things?" they asked. "And who gave you this authority?"

MATTHEW 21:23

My authority had been questioned by a five year old. I really hate it when that happens. My day had begun with "breakfast duty," the ominous task of corralling the nearly three hundred students who stream off buses and into our cafeteria for breakfast each morning. Not my idea of a fun way to start the day. I was directing students to seats abandoned by those who had already finished. A little girl with her hair in dog-ears was next in line, so I pointed her to an empty seat. The expression on her face let me know she was not a morning person.

"Who are you?" she asked with a scowl. Since I teach a specialized group of students, many of the students in our school have no idea who I am. I squatted down so that we would be face to face as I answered her question.

"My name is Mrs. Page," I said.

"Do you work here?"

"Yes."

"Are you a janitor?" she asked.

"No, I'm a teacher."

"A real teacher?" she asked, as though there might be someone running around masquerading as one.

"A real teacher," I said.

She must have decided that all of her options were shot. I did, after all, work there. I was not a janitor. Neither was I a substitute or some kind of teacher-impersonator. With an exasperated exhale that sent her bangs in a wave, she compliantly took the unwanted seat.

This miniature interrogator did not question my power to make her take that seat. I was, after all, more than twice her height and more times her weight than I want to discuss. My power to coerce her to sit where I wanted was not in question. It was my authority to redirect her plans that was being challenged.

Jesus ran into the same trouble time after time. His power was undeniable. A man who was blind was given sight. A man with leprosy was made clean. A woman with seven demons was set free. His power was demonstrated clearly and was unquestionable. His authority, however, was both a wonder and a cause for indignation. He taught "as one having authority," and yet his authority was always being questioned.

"Isn't this Joseph's son?" his challengers asked (Lk 4:22).

"Who is this fellow who speaks blasphemy?" (Lk 5:21).

"By what authority are you doing these things?" (Mt 21:23).

"You are a king, then!" (Jn 18:37).

The One whose authority is transcendent stooped down for face-to-face communication. "I AM," he said throughout the years of his earthly ministry. "I AM," he says to us today. Like the little girl with her hair in dog-ears, people today want to know if God really is who he seems to be. They want to know if he really has any business intervening in their lives. They want to know if he has any real credentials that entitle him to point them in a certain direction. Just like me, standing in the cafeteria that morning, he really is who he acts like he is, he does have the credentials, he can intervene in our lives, and even when we comply with exasperation, he will point the way.

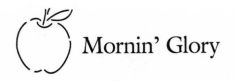

Mornin' Glory

And whoever welcomes a little child like this in my name welcomes me.

MATTHEW 18:5

On the first day of school, you see them on almost every door.

Welcome signs.

Welcome to Mrs. Thompson's class. Welcome to first grade. Welcome to senior English. Welcome back. Welcome, class of 2012.

Standing somewhere near the well-dressed door is the welcomer, usually wearing a favorite outfit, a smile, and an air of professionalism. In elementary school, those of us who have done this year after year have a few welcoming tricks up our sleeves. Lots of doors are decorated with bubble gum and candy in the morning, only to be stripped bare by midday. From day one, middle and high school teachers have the dual task of warmly welcoming their students while commanding respect. This is not an easy combination, but so important.

Welcoming the children is the first job for day one, but what happens to our welcome as the year proceeds? We slowly fade away from our doorways and retreat to our desks. Sometimes our students are greeted by nothing but the tops of our heads. We have roll to check, papers to grade, and committee reports to finish.

When I think of places where I felt welcome as a child, I

find memories that have slept awhile. I remember my next door neighbor's kitchen, where a hug and a cold biscuit with bacon awaited me each morning. I think of my fifth-grade classroom. My teacher was a rookie, a first-year teacher, but she dished out warmth and confidence like Grandma's banana pudding. Middle school is for many of us a time when we feel the least welcome in this world. But I remember one teacher on that frightening first day who chose to welcome rather than terrify her students. I remember one pair of eyes twinkling in anticipation rather than drooping in dread.

In high school, my Spanish teacher never failed to greet me with a "Buenos dias." I knew that when she also asked me how my weekend had been, she really wanted to know. More recently, Mrs. Maynard, who teaches across the hall from me, often jump-starts my day with "Mornin', Glory!" She welcomes me to glory on days that may have begun most ungloriously.

Jesus, taking a child in his arms, said, "Whoever welcomes one of these little children in my name, welcomes me."

He was simply talking about how we treat each other. When I welcome you, I celebrate your arrival. When I welcome a child in the name of Christ, I celebrate the arrival of a divine guest in my classroom. Jesus' expectation is that we will treat children the same way we would treat him. What would you do if Jesus were coming to your class today? In various forms, he will be arriving soon. Welcome him.

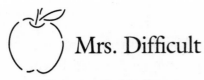

Mrs. Difficult

The Son of Man came eating and drinking, and they say, "Here is a glutton and a drunkard, a friend of tax collectors and 'sinners.'" But wisdom is proved right by her actions.

MATTHEW 11:19

My fingers were wrapped around the doorknob of the teacher's workroom when a voice behind me whispered, "I wouldn't go in there if I were you."

"Why not?"

"You-know-who is in there."

I knew who you-know-who was, and she was the last person I wanted to see on a busy Monday morning. You-know-who was one of those people one would kindly refer to as difficult. Communicating with her was difficult, getting away from a conversation with her was difficult, working with her was difficult, and finding something positive to say about her was beyond difficult. From the way she talked, one would assume there was little in this world about which she did not know something. There was much about which she knew everything. There was practically no topic about which she knew nothing, and she was compelled to share, at length, her wealth of information about everything. Wrapped around her treasury of knowledge was a storehouse of opinions, most of which were negative. You-know-who often became an uninvited third in a two-person conversation, especially since, in her opinion, her opinion was so vital.

Jesus had his share of difficult people with whom he had

to deal. The Pharisees were continually sharing with him from their wellspring of misconceptions. Other people were users who followed him around just to see the traveling miracle show or have a free fish and barley-loaf dinner. Even his own disciples were not always easy to deal with, but Jesus did not avoid engagement with difficult people. He befriended them, he confronted them, and he served them. In a nutshell, he did not give difficult people the power to be difficult.

Jesus chose to befriend a squirrelly little fellow named Zacchaeus. Tax collectors were dishonest by profession and friendless among the people. The average Harry Hebrew would have avoided Zacchaeus at all costs. Jesus, however, invited himself to lunch with the man. For difficult people, invitations are a table-turning experience; for Zacchaeus, this invitation was life-changing.

When it came to the know-it-all Pharisees, Jesus had the advantage of knowing more than they did. Over and over he used the tool of confrontation to expose their ignorance. They were upset when Jesus healed a blind man. They victimized the man who had been healed, by throwing him out of the synagogue. That was something they had the power to do. When Jesus confronted them with the truth, however, they began to argue among themselves. They were outraged that Jesus would consider them to be blind.

"What? Are we blind too?"

Jesus said, "If you were blind, you would not be guilty of sin; but now that you claim you can see, your guilt remains" (Jn 9:40-41).

Jesus' confrontation left them defenseless and arguing

among themselves. Truth disempowered their ignorance.

Of all Jesus' disciples, Peter would likely be considered the most difficult. He had a history of arguing with Jesus and thinking his motives for doing so were pure. He claimed, like one of our present-day automobile companies, to have a better idea. In John 13, when Jesus was on his knees, washing his disciples' feet, Peter tried to refuse Jesus' gift of service. Jesus served him anyway. He washed Peter's feet, knowing that later that night Peter would refuse to comfort him and would deny he even knew him. Jesus took away Peter's power to be difficult by serving him.

We, too, need to stop giving difficult people the power to be difficult. An offer of friendship diffuses destructive negativism. Mrs. Difficult can't complain that no one likes her if she is invited to join the group for lunch. Truthful confrontation disempowers ignorance. Mrs. Difficult's babbling can be silenced by, "Really? That's not my understanding at all." Opinionated misconception has no defense against truth.

I Believe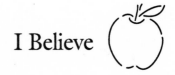

I do believe; help me overcome my unbelief!

MARK 9:24

I admit it. Sometimes it is just plain hard to believe what I believe. I believe in a sovereign God who created the universe and therefore has a right to call the shots. I believe he is a God of love and kept promises, but I also believe he is a God of wrath and carried-out threats. I believe we live in a world that is dead because of sin, but alive because of loving sacrifice. I believe that the Lord my God is One, but he is also three.

I believe that Jesus Christ is the only example of someone who has died and been resurrected, never to die again. I believe that he chose to suffer my personal punishment so that I could be united with God. I believe that he is in the Father and the Father is in him. Jesus is Lord, he suffered, and therefore he has a right to say, "I am the Way, the Truth, and the Life. No one comes to the Father except through me."

I believe that God's purpose for me, day by day and moment by moment, is to direct me to be more like Jesus. I believe that because I am called by God to that purpose, all things will work together for good. I believe that in expressing this belief, I am called upon to live it out when I encounter crisis or challenge. I believe that God would never call me to a purpose for which he would not empower me.

I believe in the indwelling Holy Spirit, who stirs, comforts, and fills me as I live in this flesh. I believe in the fellowship of that Spirit with other believers. I believe that Jesus desired unity above all else for his followers, his friends.

I believe the Evil One enjoys creating disharmony among the followers of Jesus, but I also believe that loving one another as Jesus loved us will help us to overcome the schemes of evil. I believe in forgiveness. The more I come to know my forgiven self, the more I believe in the restorative power of the good news of forgiveness. I believe we miss much if we forgive little.

I believe that believers make a difference in the world. I believe we make that difference by loving well and living in hope. I believe God is able to handle the results of every life that I touch today. I believe that because I believe, life is wonderfully beautiful and deeply mysterious. I believe and I will press on.

Scars and Stripes Forever

As obedient children, do not conform to the evil desires you had when you lived in ignorance.

1 PETER 1:14

One of my favorite scenes from the movie *Jaws* shows the old fisherman and the young scientist comparing scars. Each rolls up a sleeve or a pant leg and tries to "one-up" the other by the size of the scar or the magnitude of his pain and suffering. Most of us have played a scaled-down version of this game. We all have scars reminding us of pain suffered or lessons learned. I have a scar on the index finger of my left hand, which reminds me of the consequences of disobedience.

The first neighborhood in which I remember living was one of those postwar, frame house neighborhoods that sprang up in the early fifties. The best place to play was a fabulous ditch running behind all of the houses on our side of the street. I have no idea how deep the ditch was, but to a five year old, it was a canyon. I was allowed to play in the section of the ditch directly behind our house as long as my older brother, Terry, was along.

One summer afternoon, Terry was gone to another neighborhood to play with a friend. I was playing with a group of kids from our neighborhood. The decision was made to go to the ditch to look for arrowheads, a favorite activity of mine. I begged my mother to let me go to the ditch. Her answer was a profound "no." Convinced that my mother had no understanding of my ability to take care of myself and that what she didn't know wouldn't hurt her, I went to the ditch anyway.

My friends were having a great time picking up rocks and throwing dirt clods at each other. I would have had fun too, except for the cloud of guilt and fear hanging over my head. I stayed long enough to confirm how wrong my mother had been and decided to go home. Truthfully, I was miserable. In my hand was a coffee can rattling with potentially valuable rocks. As I climbed the tree-root ladder out of the ditch, my foot slipped and so did the coffee can. The sharp lip of the can dug deep into the tender flesh of my finger. I went crying home to my mom.

My mother stopped the bleeding and bandaged my finger. I was expecting the royal treatment, the glass-of-lemonade, sit-in-front-of-the-fan treatment. Instead, my mother cupped my face in her hands and said, "You were in the ditch, weren't you?" I knew what was next. I took my bandaged finger and my deflated ego to my room to prepare for the coming consequence.

It is hard to say which hurt the worst—my throbbing finger, my switched legs, or my stubborn pride. I learned that day that eleventh-hour repentance may not stop the natural consequences of disobedience, and that love and sympathy don't cancel promised consequences. I learned that I am not as self-sufficient as I think. Tough lessons for a five year old. Tough lessons for us all.

Legacy of Truth

I have no greater joy than to hear that my children are walking in the truth.

3 JOHN 4

The day Grandmother Page turned eighty was a day of grand celebration. Cars of every description lined the long gravel driveway leading up to her white frame farmhouse. People of equally varied descriptions filled the house and yard. Our purpose, however, was singular. We were gathered to celebrate the life of the grand matriarch of our family.

All of the uncles and a few nephews had been up all night sipping coffee, telling tales, and stoking the coals under the sacrificial hog, whose aroma assured a sumptuous barbecue feast. Heavy-eyed fire stokers took turns dozing off in their lawn chairs, their nodding heads jerking them awake with a start, always followed by adamant denials of their temporary departure.

Aunts and nieces shuttled food and flyswatters from the kitchen to the picnic tables in the backyard. Every so often one of them would tell Grandmother to go sit down and relax, an order she totally ignored. Babies napped, cried, and performed a variety of new tricks. Cousins got reacquainted. Men patted each other's shoulders and laughed. Pregnant women in various stages of ripeness patted each other's stomachs. This was a grand gathering indeed of aunts, uncles, cousins, friends, neighbors, and flies.

Finally, the table was laid, the blessing prayed, and the feasting began. One yard-full of people consumed half a hog, twelve fried chickens, ninety-six ears of corn, eight pounds of sliced tomatoes, nine bowls of potato salad, six bowls of peas, three trays of baked beans, and more potato chips than could be counted, along with fresh green beans, hot rolls, and one well-lighted birthday cake. We each made a contribution to the feast that day, in honor of a lady who had given something of herself to all of us.

Late in the afternoon, as the feasting settled into fellowship, I saw Grandmother seated in a lawn chair under a gigantic tree in the front yard. Two of her grown granddaughters were positioned at her feet, enjoying her company, listening to her wisdom. I thought of all she had passed on to her children, grandchildren, and great-grandchildren. Her eyes have smiled at me from a younger face— that of her grandson. I had heard her laugh in the kitchen that morning, in the voice of one of her children. My son Michael is a left-handed pitcher thanks to her. Her tender touch with a garden, her love of a hard day's work, her loyalty to family, all found their way into the lives of those who surrounded her. But far more important than blue eyes or laughter or a gardener's touch, to all of us who celebrated her that day, she had passed on the truth. Anyone who was in her presence knew that she was a daughter of God and that she loved her Father very much.

She looked like a queen seated on her throne that summer afternoon, beginning her ninth decade with honor and joy, and I wondered what went through her mind as she surveyed her lineage all gathered together. I am sure she was proud. I know she felt loved and honored. But her greatest joy must have been in knowing that her children were connected by the truth. As I observed her reign I prayed that I would know that same joy, the joy of knowing that my children were walking in truth.

End Controlled Access

Today, if you hear his voice, do not harden your hearts as you did in the rebellion.

HEBREWS 3:7-8

Driving down a familiar highway, I noticed a sign I had never seen before. Maybe it was a new sign. Maybe I was simply less distracted than usual. "END CONTROLLED ACCESS," it read in bold black on yellow. Until then, I had not even noticed that I was on a controlled-access highway, though it had certainly made driving easier.

A controlled-access highway provides me with a certain level of security as a driver. I don't have to worry about being surprised by a car whipping into my path from my blind side. I am notified of exits and on-ramps miles before I reach them. I know when to expect intrusion, when to change lanes, and when to use cruise control. Helpful road signs matter-of-factly and unemotionally inform me of my choices along the way. Limited-access roads provide a pre-dictability to the traffic flow, so I do not need to fear what is beyond the next hill. Traveling down a controlled-access highway, I feel safe, protected, and confident.

The message on the sign that day did not set me to thinking about speed limits and passing lanes, however. The message that day was for my soul: "Linda, END CON-TROLLED ACCESS."

When it comes to controlled and limited access to my soul, I am an expert. I don't like surprises or being blindsided, so I prefer to determine the location and timing of the exits and on-ramps to my emotional self. I decide when you may intrude into my thoughts and feelings and when you may not.

CONTROLLED ACCESS.

Sometimes I find myself on cruise control, looking to neither the left nor the right, and certain of my ability to plow through whatever is ahead.

CONTROLLED ACCESS.

With my body language or attitude, I can say "Exit Now," while simultaneously my silent soul is screaming, "Please come closer!" If you go, you will, after all, only be following the signs. CONTROLLED ACCESS. I will ignore the truth that the highway I travel has far more to offer than simply being a means of moving from point A to point B. Though beauty lines the highway and you may want to share it with me, I will press on blindly to point B. CONTROLLED ACCESS.

God has challenged me to exit my safe, predictable highway. He has challenged me to risk taking the scenic route, where the intrusion of relationship lies beyond the next hill. I am venturing out more and more. It's risky. I'm learning. God grant me the courage to ... END CONTROLLED ACCESS.

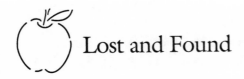 Lost and Found

Whoever finds his life will lose it, and whoever loses his life for my sake will find it.

MATTHEW 10:39

Gwen loses her life four times a week. Each afternoon, Monday through Thursday, after teaching fifth grade all day long, she goes to the Boys and Girls Club and volunteers her time as a tutor. For ninety minutes a day, she puts her wants, her needs, her life on hold and gives it to the youngsters at the Boys and Girls Club. She loses her life and finds it again in the eyes of children.

Bob loses his life three days at a time. Four times a year, he spends a weekend involved in prison ministry. He leaves his home, his family, his job as a school superintendent, and all of the things that demand his time, giving himself to men seeking hope. When the prison doors clang shut, he loses his life. No one within the prison walls knows that he has a Ph.D. No one calls him "Doctor" or sees the kind of car he drives. He loses his life but finds it pulsing in the hearts of men who become new creations.

Maria loses her life bit by bit. Almost every day, she spends time with AIDS victims in a hospice not far from her home. Maria's brother died of AIDS four years ago, and she knows its destructive power all too well. She is determined that as this disease takes the bodies of these precious men and women, it will take neither their humanity nor their hope. It will not steal their dignity or drain away their hearts. She takes walks with these men and women. She shares her faith with them, watches movies and eats popcorn with them, prays with them, and loves them. When one of her friends loses life, she loses part of hers, but she has found a fire inside of her that she did not know was there. She loses her life only to find it again in her passion to give it away.

Jesus said, "Whoever loses his life for my sake will find it." Many a martyr has given his life for the cause of Christ. I do not know if I will be called upon to die for my faith, but I am surely called upon to lose my life. Losing my life means I have to come face to face with the worthlessness of all that I own, the value of who I am, the price of grace, and the holiness of my God. It is in thus finding my life that I am willing to lose. It is in losing that I find. Only a life that is given away is one that is truly found.

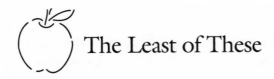

The Least of These

I was hungry and you gave me something to eat, I was thirsty and you gave me something to drink, I was a stranger and you invited me in, I needed clothes and you clothed me, I was sick and you looked after me, I was in prison and you came to visit me.

MATTHEW 25:35-36

"All she does is use up air and take up space. She can't do anything. She acts retarded." These stinging, worth-shattering words about one of my learning-disabled students came streaming from the heart of her classroom teacher. I stood speechless and stunned by the fiery tirade. I am usually ready with one of my "Every Kid Is Different" speeches, but this time I had been caught completely off guard and the teacher knew it.

She had her say and left my room in a huff, leaving me to absorb what I had just heard. This veteran teacher had judged my student unworthy of the air she breathed and incapable of doing anything worthwhile. Because of this youngster's behavior more than because of her academics, her teacher chose to label her "retarded."

As the door to my classroom quietly closed, I felt a sense of total despair. How could I fight an attitude that gave so little value to the life of a child? How could I teach a teacher who was herself unteachable? Would one so quick to judge and with so hard a heart ever be willing to love a child with a "difference"? The words of Jesus resounded in my head: "Anything you did to the least of these, you have done to me." I was fighting in this teacher an attitude bent on keeping the "least of these" exactly that: with the least value, the least purpose, and the least sense of belonging and worth.

Some people have to make a special effort to come in contact with the "least of these," but we teachers have a ready-made supply. We don't have to go to a soup kitchen or a homeless shelter to find them. We don't have to wait for the ringing bells of Christmas to be reminded that even our nation is filled with people of great need. The "least of these" walk through the doors of our classrooms every day. It doesn't matter if you teach special education in an economically deprived area or honors algebra in an exclusive private school. The "least of these" are there.

Some are hungry for food, some for attention. Some are imprisoned by abuse, some by loneliness, some by bodies and minds that don't work just right. Though none are naked, many are cold.

We can warm them or leave them shivering. We can soothe them with "cool water" or chide them with sarcasm. We can visit them in their prisons or ignore them in their quietness. What a privilege to have them in our classrooms. What an honor to minister to Christ himself. Lord, give us eyes to see and hearts to know you as the "least of these."

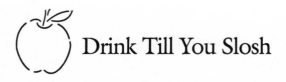# Drink Till You Slosh

As the deer pants for streams of water, so my soul pants for you, O God.

PSALM 42:1

The summer of 1980 was the hottest, driest summer that I can remember. The temperature broke 100 degrees day after day, accompanied by stifling humidity. Why in the world I decided to run a 10-K race on the Fourth of July, I cannot remember, but I ran it. The race was set for 8:30 in the morning, which meant that the temperature was a cool 89 degrees at the starting gun. The humidity was graciously only 95 percent. The sun was radiating its best on 6.2 miles of totally unshaded, unlevel highway, and I was out there, unbelievably, by choice.

The halfway point was the one and only water stop. I drank one cupful and poured another on my head as I trotted on. I could feel my skin temperature rising, and by the time I climbed the last hill at the finish line, my heart was pounding in my ears. I was just beginning to experience the effects of dehydration.

Usually, in those days, a six-mile run left me energized and relaxed. Not this one. For the three days following the race, my legs felt like they belonged to someone else, and I was forced to drag them along. My mouth was constantly thirsty—not dry, just thirsty. All I wanted to do was rest and drink, drink, drink. I would drink until I sloshed, but I was still thirsty. I now have an understanding of the term "unquenchable thirst."

In the culture in which Jesus lived, water was life. Historically, the Hebrew people were nomadic, desert people, who knew from experience the value of water. In that culture, when a guest entered your home, your first gesture of hospitality was to offer him or her a drink of water. The question, "Are you thirsty?" was unnecessary. Perhaps the people of the Bible lived their lives with a continuous thirst on their lips.

Jesus was speaking to thirsty people in the seventh chapter of John when he said, "If anyone is thirsty, let him come to me and drink." Most of us know what it is like to see a television advertisement for an icy, dripping, bubbling cola when we are thirsty. We head immediately for the kitchen. In the same way Jesus beckons us, with his own version of a "springs of living water" commercial.

In a culture where water is readily available, Jesus would have us live with a continuous thirst on our lips—a thirst to know him. Like my three days of unquenchable thirst, we are to drink until we slosh, but still want more. Perhaps our first act of hospitality to those we meet should be to offer them a spiritual drink of water. The question, "Are you thirsty?" is unnecessary.

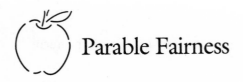 Parable Fairness

Well done, good and faithful servant! You have been faithful with a few things; I will put you in charge of many things. Come and share your master's happiness.

Matthew 25:23

In a conversation, my friend Jan was lamenting the departure of a fine young teacher leaving our school to pursue his doctorate.

"He was so good with my son, Jimmy," Jan said. "He knew that Jimmy had some learning problems, so Mr. Yelverton just figured out how to teach him. He discovered that Jimmy was an auditory learner, so the day before the final exam, he invited Jimmy over to his house to study the material aloud. Mr. Yelverton is a teacher who knows that everyone has different abilities and he teaches to students' strengths."

What a conviction against those who think that being fair means treating everyone the same! In the parable of the talents, we see the paradoxical but true meaning of fairness. In the story, the master of the house was leaving on a trip. Before leaving, he doled out responsibility for his money to his servants, "each according to his ability." No one protested, "That's not fair!" The master left each servant with the responsibility that was exactly suitable for him.

Upon the master's return, each servant was expected to have done well. The servant who had been left with five talents had doubled his master's money. The master's response was a first-century version of "I knew you could do it!" The servant who had been given two talents got a "Hebrew high five" and a "Let's have a party!" Servant number three was the one who found trouble.

Servant number three had been given one talent, according to his ability, and he had done absolutely nothing with his master's money. He had buried it and returned it to the master. Was the master happy to have his money back? No, he was furious. He called servant number three a lazy, no-good bum and threw him out on his ear.

Until my conversation with Jan about Jimmy and Mr. Yelverton, I had always looked for myself in one of the servants in the parable of the talents. The question I had asked myself was, "Am I doing my best with what God has given me?" Now, however, I see myself as the master in the story, and I am intruded upon by an entirely different set of questions. Do I really know my students and fully understand their abilities? Do I treat them with "parable fairness"? Do I really praise, reward, and celebrate a job well done? If a student does in fact have only a small amount of ability, do I hide him away and pass him on unchanged? Or do I teach him in the way he can learn and show him high expectations?

I pray that I will know my students and teach them fairly, that I will expect their best and celebrate it. I pray that at year's end we will embrace the work we have done and say, "Let's have a party!"

I Almost Missed It

She has done a beautiful thing to me.

MARK 14:6

I almost missed it. My friend, Bekah, and I were out for a walk on a gorgeous spring afternoon. We had not visited in several days, so we were furiously playing catch-up in our conversation. Suddenly, in mid-sentence she took my arm, stopped my stride, and whispered, "Look, the yellow finches are here."

I was vaguely aware of the fluttering yellow dots on the ground ahead. I guess I thought they were dandelions blowing in the breeze. Then a wave of yellow speckles left the ground, did a synchronized swoop in front of us, and disappeared in the trees. My eyes were opened to hundreds of the tiny birds on the ground, in the air, and in the trees. They reacted little to our presence, but we were amazed by theirs. They were here only for the night, a stopover in their migration, and I had almost missed their visit. If not for Bekah's staying hand and quiet whisper, I would have missed something beautiful.

Just prior to my senior year in high school, a new friend moved to town from Grand Island, Nebraska. One fall afternoon, Emmy rode with me to my grandparents' house in the country. We traveled along gravel roads, shaded over by giant oak, elm, and sweet gum trees. Emmy twisted and turned in the front seat of the car, looking out every window. She had never seen so many trees so close together and so alive with color. The trees were welcoming us dressed in their fall finery. If not for Emmy's wide-eyed wonder, I would have missed something beautiful.

Only once during his ministry did Jesus describe something as "beautiful." He was attending a celebration dinner following the resurrection of Lazarus. Party noise and chatter filled the room, when the celebrants noticed a powerful aroma.

The sweet fragrance drew all eyes to Mary, Lazarus' sister, kneeling before Jesus. She had broken open her personal bottle of burial perfume, worth thousands of dollars, and had poured it on Jesus' feet. Her hair served as her towel.

What followed was one of those frozen moments when no one knows quite what to do or say. A woman had no business in the room with the men, she had let down her hair in public, and she had completely wasted a valuable bottle of perfume. Maybe the disciples remembered that Jesus had defended Mary in the past, so in their wisdom, they decided to point out to the Son of God that she had been wasteful.

Jesus' response? He told them to leave her alone. A beautiful act of sacrificial worship was taking place right before their eyes and they had missed it. They saw what she did. They drank in the aroma of the perfume, but they missed the beauty. They missed seeing Mary's heart. Jesus saw and called it beautiful.

I wonder what I missed yesterday. Did I overlook a scene in creation that would inspire an artist's brush? Did an act of kindness, of service, or of worship take place right before my eyes? Take my arm, Lord, break my stride, turn my head, and whisper to me.

# Giants

I thank my God every time I remember you.

PHILIPPIANS 1:3

Don Quixote mistook windmills for them. A green one has sold countless green beans. The Bible says that they might have been real. Your mother probably told you they don't exist, but the National Basketball Association has evidence to the contrary. To someone, you probably are one.

"They" are giants. I believe in them. I have known a few in my life, though not the "fe, fi, fo, fum" kind. They were not giants in linear measure, but rather in the measure of their character and impact on my life. My grandmother, my father's mother, was one of my giants.

She stood no more than five feet, two inches tall, five feet, three at the most. She was a bit broader than she should have been, but then a girlish figure was the last thing on her mind.

My grandmother told me stories. Stories of growing up poor, of strumming the guitar in accompaniment with her father's fiddle at the local hotel, of teaching school—"all eight grades"—in a one-room schoolhouse, of my father's childhood antics, of a mother's love and the emptiness left by the loss of a child.

"There is no love like a mother's love," she told me.

Twenty years after her death, I finally understand. I can still see her stooping down to fit me into a dress or a blouse she had made for me. Sometimes when I laugh, I hear her.

Grandmother always had corn on the table for me and cornbread for my dad. She was the master of her kitchen and happiest when we were all clamoring for a taste of fried chicken or a finger-full of mashed potatoes. When she talked to me, she was always smoothing my blouse or straightening my collar. Not that she was so much concerned with my appearance, but touching me seemed important.

Riding in the backseat of the car with her one day, I remember investigating the wonders of her hands.

"My hands used to look just like yours," she said.

"Impossible," I thought, for my hands were smooth and unspotted. Yet, a replica of her hands now transfers these thoughts to paper. She gave me my first glimpse of the reality that aging was as surely in my future as youth was in her past.

Grandmother stood straight and proud. Only grief, inescapable grief, stooped her shoulders. But even in the helplessness of sorrow, she was larger than life to me.

> I believe in giants,
> I have known a few.
> To someone,
> A giant
> Is you.

 Worth It All

Whatever you do, work at it with all your heart, as working for the Lord, not for men.

COLOSSIANS 3:23

I can still see him as he walked into my resource class that first day—neatly dressed, every hair in place except for a stubborn cowlick on the left side of his forehead, a typical second-grade boy. He slumped into a seat near the front and sat with knees up and head bowed.

His body language revealed his thoughts: "Maybe if I can't see her, she won't see me."

I purposefully walked over and stood near him as I greeted "old-timers" returning for another year. Placing my hand on his shoulder, I said, "It's nice to have you."

He turned his eyes toward mine and whispered, "I can't read."

"I know," I whispered in response. "None of these fellas could last year, either. We'll do everything we can to fix it."

I'm not sure he believed me at the time. At the ripe old age of eight, he had already learned to expect failure in school. He had learned to anticipate ridicule from his class-mates. He had learned to expect little to make sense and much to bring confusion. And so we set to work, that little man, his classmates and I.

It was so very hard for him at first. We took a different approach to reading, and I know that it seemed a little like starting all over to him. But little by little, confusion gave way to revelation, and he began to "get it." He no longer sat all folded up in his chair hoping no one would notice him. He became "one of the guys," laughing and talking and even trying my patience occasionally when it was time to get serious.

Nine years have passed since that initial whispered conversation. Today's mail brought a well-written, perfectly punctuated letter from a teenage boy who I happen to know still has a stubborn cowlick. His letter requested a recommendation from me to help him complete the requirements for his Eagle Scout award.

He is taller than I am now, broad-shouldered, manly. I see him occasionally, and his eyes greet mine with confidence, followed by a beaming smile. He is doing very well in school these days. College and a bright future await him.

I wish he knew what his confidence means to me, how his smile warms my heart, how his future gives me hope. I pray that he never loses the drive and desire that pushed him to learn when learning was so hard. I pray that I never lose the perseverance to do everything I can to pull the future closer for my students. They are worth the shrill of a 5:30 A.M. alarm and the vibrating nerves it brings. They are worth it all.

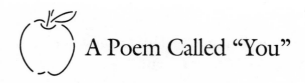 A Poem Called "You"

For we are God's workmanship, created in Christ Jesus to do good works, which God prepared in advance for us to do.

EPHESIANS 2:10

We do not wonder so much at ourselves anymore. I am amazed at how content our world has become with allowing computers, telescopes, and radio waves to tell us who we are and where we have come from. It is all so calculated, so numerical, so incidental. Compliant heads nod in agreement when some new theory of how we all came to be makes the headlines.

Scientists, brilliant people, educated people, would have us believe that the rhythm, the rhyme, and the harmony of the earth's waking and sleeping were all made possible by a series of cosmic collisions. They say that somewhere in the neighborhood of 4.56 billion years ago, particles of cosmic dust began slamming into each other and sticking together until earth happened. Then at some point, in a gigantic, celestial whoops-a-daisy, something smashed into the stuck-together ball and tilted it on its axis. Suddenly, there was exactly enough warmth to germinate tulips in Holland and corn in Nebraska. Then one day, out of a wet, murky warmth somewhere, crawled a creature that would evolve into Neanderthal Man, Albert Einstein, the kid next door, and you.

Sudden accidental incidents giving birth to our planet and to all its inhabitants leaves out the creative, imaginative hand of God. The idea that all that is beautiful, colorful, and delightful, all that is kind, loving, and forgiving, came into being incidentally is beyond my comprehension.

God would have us know that we, the people of the earth, are his "workmanship." Literally translated, the word for "workmanship" means "poem" or "masterpiece." Think on that for a moment. We are God's poem. We are not just a work completed and found adequate, certainly not some cosmic typo, but a rhythmic, lyrical composition designed with purpose and meaning.

Poets express the inexpressible. They find the unsearchable places of my soul, spread them before me, and invite me to know myself. They see unspeakable beauty that eludes my eye, and call me to observe my world. They point out the absurdities of life and help me laugh at my failures and vanities. But far more than any of this, poets dare to expose their very own hearts and allow me to know them.

God desired to express the inexpressible, so he wrote a poem called "Me" and another one called "You" and "You" and "You." Each person is a poem, each life an anthology. Dare to examine and to risk understanding the poem that is "You." Dare to read and risk loving the one called "Me." In so doing, you will find peace, and even more you will find the Poet himself.

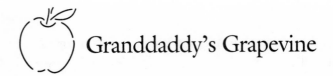

Granddaddy's Grapevine

I am the vine; you are the branches. If a man remains in me and I in him, he will bear much fruit; apart from me you can do nothing.

JOHN 15:5

Every summer I have a craving for big, juicy, black grapes. It's a holdover from my childhood that just will not go away. My grandfather was a master gardener. He managed to grow fabulous vegetables in the puniest sandy soil in the world. I will never know how he did it. He grew tomatoes, beans, corn, peas, peppers, and the world's best peanuts.

Probably the most prolific plant in the garden was a monster grapevine that grew along one entire side of the toolshed. My grandfather strung wire fencing from the roof of the toolshed to the top of the garden fence, about ten feet away. The grapevine stretched its arms up the side of the toolshed, entwined and wrapped itself in the fencing overhead, and came back down the garden fencerow. The result was a natural tunnel made of grapevine and grape leaves.

In late summer the walls and ceiling of the leaf-tunnel hung heavy with juicy, black grapes. No cake and cookies for me, thank you. Give me grapes, lots of sweet, juicy grapes. My brother, my cousins, and I would stand and eat every grape within our reach, barely impacting the bountiful supply. Grandmother made grape jelly and grape juice.

We took home sacks full of grapes so my mother could do the same. My aunts and my grandparents' neighbors had all the grapes they wanted. All of the yards and yards of grapevine seemed happy to provide.

Every grapevine branch and every pound of grapes from my grandfather's garden grew from a single vine. No wonder I had no trouble understanding what Jesus meant when he said, "I am the vine and my Father is the gardener.... I am the vine and you are the branches."

I saw how from a single seed had grown a vine as big around as my grandfather's arm. From it grew hundreds of feet of branches, stretching up, over, and down. Every healthy branch that drew water and nutrition from the vine was teeming with gifts of sweet, delicious fruit. All a branch had to do to be a fruit bearer was to stay connected to the vine.

Jesus asks little more of us, his branches. He asks us to stay connected in order to bear fruit. He put it quite simply: "Apart from me you can do nothing." Surely then, the opposite must also be true. Connected to him, you can do much. As for those branches that don't bear any fruit, they are good for nothing but firewood. Stay connected, fellow branches, and we will bear our own delicious fruit.

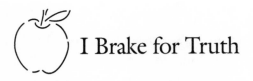

I Brake for Truth

Join with others in following my example, brothers, and take note of those who live according to the pattern we gave you.

PHILIPPIANS 3:17

My sons and I were stuck in construction traffic—one of the benefits of living in a booming small city. Michael, my thirteen year old, started a conversation with his brother.

"Did you see what Alicia did at lunch today?"

"Yeah, how stupid can you get?"

"What happened?" I asked, not really liking the direction the discussion was headed.

"You should have seen it, Mom," answered Jeff, my fifteen year old. "She put a sandwich wrapped in foil in the microwave and pow, pow, pow! It started popping and flashing. I thought it was gonna blow the door off the microwave. The whole place cracked up. What a dufus!"

"Yeah," added Michael, "what an idiot!"

"Hold it right there, guys. What's this name-calling bit?" I asked as traffic finally edged along. I wasn't especially in a hurry, but the driver ahead of me needed some encouragement. Honk! Honk! "Come on, Granny, green means go."

"Mom, nobody with any sense would put aluminum foil in the microwave," said Jeff.

"I think I've done it myself a few times, and I don't think it gives you the right to degrade my character or my intelligence," I replied. "I really hate it when you guys call people names and make judgments about them just because of a simple mistake."

My mind was racing through all of the reasons why my sons would stoop to this behavior. Maybe it was too much TV. Maybe it was those programs where the plot is to see who could insult whom the most. Maybe we shouldn't have missed the Family Life Conference at church. Maybe ...

"Wow!" I shrieked. "Did you see that idiot turn right from the left lane? How do these people get a driver's license? Anyway, haven't you guys learned anything about valuing people simply as God's creations? What about building people up, rather than tearing them down? What if Alicia had already had a bad day? How do you think the rest of her day went, after the whole cafeteria laughed at her?"

We were finally moving along at a decent pace. I thought I had done a fair job of lecturing on the value of human life.

"Mom," said Jeff, pointing out the driver-side window. "That guy wants into our lane."

"I know," I said. "I hate it when people do that. Why should I let him in? The signs have been saying 'Left Lane Ends' for the last two miles."

"Maybe he has an emergency. Maybe he can't read. Maybe he's just had a bad day."

I put on my brakes in more ways than one.

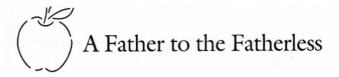 A Father to the Fatherless

A father to the fatherless, a defender of widows, is God in his holy dwelling.

PSALM 68:5

There have been a few times in my career when I have disagreed with disciplinary actions taken or not taken by a principal. I have learned to quietly accept decisions I cannot change. Sometimes I have even come to see the wisdom in disciplinary choices that I at first thought unwise.

Cassandra was sent to the office for using foul language in her fifth-grade class. A few weeks earlier she had done the same thing in my room. Our guidance counselor was trying to help her with her word choices. So far, nothing had made much difference.

Cassandra was a physically mature fifth-grade girl whose intellectual functioning was borderline. Her mother worked nights at a convenience store. At night, Cassandra stayed at home with her older sister, her sister's baby, and one younger sister. Cassandra's father was a drug addict who had never lived with the family. When it came to advantages, Cassandra had none.

Some of Cassandra's behaviors that went unchecked at home were not acceptable at school. She couldn't throw used tissues on the floor, spit in the wastebasket, or shriek profanity in class. We were making progress on the first two, but the language situation kept arising. Consequently, Cassandra made her way down the hall to the principal's office.

Our principal was a kind man, but when necessary he could strike fear in the hearts of children. I happened to be standing in the outer office when the principal's door opened and out walked Cassandra smiling. Mr. Ray saw me and motioned me into his office.

"What did you say to her?" I asked.

He turned around with a twinkle in his eye and said, "I told her she was pretty."

"You told her what?"

"I told her she was too pretty to use ugly language."

"You didn't put the fear in her?"

"No."

"Didn't tell her she was on a fast train to jail?"

"Nope, I just told her she was pretty." He was grinning.

I didn't question him out loud, but inside, my brain was churning. "Great! He told her she was pretty. I've got 'Miss North Elementary School' in class next hour, filthy mouth and all."

I returned to class fully expecting Cassandra to give a profanity lesson to anyone who would listen, but she didn't, not that day, or for several weeks after. Each day, Mr. Ray would make a point of greeting her in the hall and telling any teacher he saw how proud he was of Cassandra.

Nancy Groom, an author and speaker, tells us that little girls' daughter-souls yearn to see their father's eyes light up when they enter a room.*

When we gave a letter-writing assignment in fifth-grade English, Cassandra wrote to Mr. Ray. With misspelled words and terrible grammar, she apologized for being "bad" and thanked him for being the nicest person in the world. Mr. Ray had made a father-connection with a daughter-soul that was wasting away. Wisdom looks beyond the "said" and the "did" and finds the need.

*Nancy Groom, *Heart to Heart About Men* (Colorado Springs: NavPress, 1995), 39.

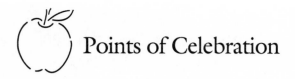 Points of Celebration

Be devoted to one another in brotherly love. Honor one another above yourselves.

ROMANS 12:10

"Come on. Let's celebrate!" "This calls for a celebration!" "He is a highly celebrated writer and authority."

The word "celebrate" calls to mind such high and positive emotion. I think of streamers, party hats, cake, reception lines, food, bubbling fountains of champagne, music, lifted glasses, food, dancing feet, silliness, and food. I have celebrated weddings, graduations, birthdays, homecomings, reunions, promotions, anniversaries, births, victories, bon voyages, beginnings, and endings.

Though we name our celebrations by event, we really celebrate people. On your birthday, I celebrate you and honor your life, not the day. The same is true for weddings, anniversaries, comings, goings, and all our celebrations. We celebrate people. My friend Dr. Kathy Koch has a ministry, called Celebrate Kids, Inc., whose mission is to remind us that children and young people need to be, and should be, celebrated just for who they are.

I work with youngsters every day who have never lacked for celebration. They have been honored with trophies, parties, gifts, balloons, flowers, visits from grandparents, limousine rides, and whatever else the creative minds of their parents can conjure. There are others who have known no celebration. Their entry into the world may have been an unwelcome event, or the struggles of life may simply weigh too heavily upon those who would celebrate.

We all seek to be celebrated. That is why it sometimes falls to us as teachers to find "points of celebration" in our students.* Even those with the least amount of celebrity have points of celebration, and as we discover them, we can bring about change in a youngster's life. How would James' life be changed if he received the following note from his history teacher?

Dear James,
I celebrate you today. I saw you walk away from a confrontation yesterday. That took courage. Thanks to your decision, no one was hurt. You are growing to be a strong man. Here's to you, James.

Mrs. Hemrick

Or what if Beth found a happy-face-shaped note on her desk?

Hey, Beth!
That top you are wearing today is your color! It makes your eyes sparkle, especially when you smile. Here's to you, Beth!

Mrs. Aldrich

We can find points of celebration in all of our students, as well as in our friends, our colleagues, and our family members. By discovering points of celebration, we can change someone's day or even someone's life. Here's to you this day for seeking points of celebration!

---

*I'm borrowing this phrase from a sermon given by Dr. Richard Allen Farmer at Evangelical Community Church in Jackson, Tennessee, May 26, 1997.

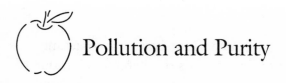

Pollution and Purity

Blessed are the pure in heart, for they will see God.

MATTHEW 5:8

When you hear the word "pure," what images come to your mind? An Egyptian treasure made of pure gold? A perfect diamond? An ice-cold glass of spring water? When I think of pure, I think of the resonant sound of a single violin played with masterful perfection in an empty concert hall. To me, that is purity.

We live in a world filled with pollutants, poisons, imperfections, and intrusions. Purity of anything seems ever harder to find. We filter, inspect, strain, distill, mix down, refine, homogenize, and pasteurize, and still impurities intrude. I am glad that when Jesus was passing out blessings in his Sermon on the Mount, he did not say, "Blessed are the pure," but instead, "Blessed are the pure in heart." A state of purity sounds like a lot of work. A state of purity of heart sounds like an act of grace.

Sometimes, to understand the meaning of a concept, we have to look at its opposite. I saw the opposite of pure as I was walking down a country road one summer afternoon. I came to a pond that was covered with a thick film of green scum. Old cola cans protruded from the water's edge. Someone had been using this pond as a garbage dump, and the stench was disgusting. The water was still and rancid. Nothing could draw life from this cesspool of pollution.

Neither does a polluted heart give life. From a polluted

heart flow messages of selfishness and bitterness that smother and suffocate life. The waters of a polluted heart are still and unchanging. The stench from such a heart warns all to stay away.

"That's just the way I am," says my polluted, unchanging heart. "I'm comfortable in my misery. Besides, I tried stirring around once and it hurt."

"Come to me," says the One who purifies, "and I will give you springs of living water."

I can no more purify my own heart than I could create an underground stream to purify the old pond. David, the psalmist, understood his inability to purify his own heart. "Create in me a pure heart, O God," he wrote (Ps 51:10), for out of his heart had come only pollution. David knew that God and only God could restore the joy that comes from a pure heart.

A pure heart is a flowing, life-giving stream. Those who come near it are refreshed and renewed. A pure heart is a heart that belongs to Christ. Blessed are the pure in heart—those whose hearts are Christ's—for they shall see God.

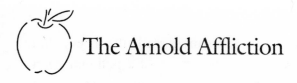

The Arnold Affliction

"I know the plans I have for you," declares the Lord, "plans to prosper you and not to harm you, plans to give you hope and a future."

JEREMIAH 29:11

He's coming and there is nothing you can do about it. He's the kid nobody wants. The one everyone prays that some other teacher will get. His reputation is one that you wouldn't believe if you didn't know for a fact it was all true.

His kindergarten teacher took early retirement the year after she had him. His first-grade teacher jumped up and kissed the doctor when she was told she needed back surgery. His second-grade teacher moved to another state and cut all ties with your school.

Now it's your turn. The principal was quite fair in her method of choosing a teacher for Arnold, also known as "The Terminator." She used the old method of drawing straws, holding the straw-drawing ceremony on the last day of school. You picked the wrong day to rely upon the powers of your unconscious mind to help you find the long straw. You reached in and pulled out a straw that was no more than a half-inch long. The principal tenderly placed Arnold's file in your hands while the other teachers were high-fiving each other.

Most of us have spent at least one summer with an "Arnold cloud" hanging over our heads. It's enough to take the lullaby out of the ocean waves or the whisper out of the mountain breeze. My friend Sandy tells of a year when six—yes, six—little first-grade Arnolds took their places in her classroom.

Sandy's summer had been a time of adjustments beyond anything she could have imagined because her husband died just after school was out. Whenever her mind drifted forward to the school year, she was confident that God was going to give her an easy class. Sandy knew that she would be the classroom teacher for one of my special education students. That was manageable, since with him came a personal assistant. What she didn't know was that occupying six other desks in her classroom were the most at-risk boys in the entire first grade.

These boys needed all Sandy had to give and more. They needed instruction, correction, and direction. They needed to be seated. They needed encouragement, consistency, firmness, and love.

God knew when he placed Trevor and his assistant in Sandy's room that six little boys needed to be in a situation where a back would never be turned on them. Between Sandy and Peggy, the assistant, at least two eyes were looking at the six boys at all times. Those little Arnolds were loved and cared for like six little angels. Sandy knows that God ordained that year especially for her.

There is no doubt that those boys needed Sandy, but she needed them also. She needed to spend the year working and giving as she had never done before. She needed to depend on the Lord as she had never done before.

So when you draw the short straw, when Arnold (or Arnold-times-six) walks through your door, remember Sandy. Arnold may need you, but even more, you may need Arnold.

 Close Calls

What man can live and not see death, or save himself from the power of the grave?

PSALM 89:48

I have never served on the front lines of battle, or been told by a doctor that he could make no promises for my life. I have not had to find the courage to draw a line in the sand and dare death to cross. But three times one summer, twice in one day, I danced with death and was given release from its grasp.

Danger did not cross my mind as I was driving home from Tupelo, Mississippi, one summer afternoon. My son Jeff, exhausted from a golf tournament, slept soundly in the backseat. My friend Bekah was keeping me company on the two-hour drive.

Mine was the lead car at a stoplight when red blinked to green. I eased forward, looking both ways. Turning my attention ahead, I saw a blur in front of me. A blue truck came from my left, through the intersection at highway speed. How he missed me I will never know. My heart leapt into my throat, I slammed on my brakes, and the blue blur disappeared down the street. I couldn't speak. Bekah uttered, "Thank you, God," and on we drove, dazed, amazed, and thankful to be alive.

Fifty or so miles down the highway, I topped a hill to find a large, black, luxury car coming straight at me in my lane. The highway was being widened, and the only place I had to go was a soft, rutted, gravel shoulder. Off-road I went, at sixty miles per hour. We washboarded on the shoulder for what seemed like a slow-motion eternity and somehow returned to the highway. I remember looking heavenward and saying, "What?" Bekah and I talked the rest of the way home—and for days afterward—about what could have happened but didn't, what should have happened but wasn't allowed.

My third brush with death that summer happened in the midst of a phone conversation. I knew a storm was approaching and that I should hang up soon. My son Michael called my name from upstairs. As I set the phone on the counter the sound of a thousand shotguns exploded around me, and blue fire shot from the earpiece. Lightning had struck the roof of our house just above where the boys were playing. No one was hurt, and the resulting fire snuffed itself out inside the wall.

After the fire trucks and the neighbors had all left, I had time to ponder my close call. Mostly I thought about how often we unknowingly teeter between life and death. Another inch, another second, a receiver to my ear, and the outcome of any of these circumstances would have been different. I now have a different perspective on just how fragile life is. I have a deeper gratitude for each breath. I have a greater desire to do whatever God has called me to do with each day. May I remember with close-call urgency to value every minute of every day.

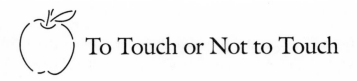 To Touch or Not to Touch

And all who touched him were healed.

MATTHEW 14:36

"Remember last week when we talked about good touches and bad touches?" I heard the guidance counselor say as I walked past a kindergarten classroom. Twenty-five little heads nodded in reply. "Today we're going to talk about how good touches and bad touches can come from the same person."

Good touches and bad touches have always existed, but we have identified them as such only in recent years. In so doing, we protect our innocents, but sometimes I wonder how much farther the pendulum can swing.

During the same week that I overheard our guidance counselor speaking about touches, national newspapers publicized the story of a six-year-old boy, and my local newspaper carried the story of a coach. Accusations of sexual harassment were levied upon both. Suddenly, a kindergartner's kiss on the cheek is added to the list of bad touches, and because of accusations only, a fabulous coach will coach no more. The pendulum rides high. I have some students who shrink away from a touch on the shoulder and others who wrap a long arm around my shoulders and pull me close. I do not want to offend or reject anyone.

The power of the human touch is extraordinary. Touches can be refreshing, reassuring, healing, and tender. They can also be painful and revolting. A small number of true offenders who should never have been allowed in the classroom have forever damaged the trust and privilege of touch for all of us.

Jesus was a toucher. The Gospels tell us that he called the children to come to him and he took them in his arms. He touched blind eyes and gave sight, leprous skin and made it clean, lifeless bodies and gave them breath. On the night of his betrayal, Jesus washed his disciples' feet, touching not just their uncleanness but their reluctance with his love. Jesus never used his hands to hurt, never drew back his fist, never brought down the back of his hand. The sight of Jesus' hands moving toward a person was always welcome and comforting.

What about us as teachers in this day of lawsuits and media blitz? Do we give up touching altogether? Do we deny our students the reassurance of a hand on the shoulder, the tenderness of a needed hug? Do we respond to fear or reach out with love?

I say we offer our touches. We touch tenderly, we touch publicly, but we touch. We dare not relinquish this vital communication tool. We dare not be less than Jesus himself showed us to be. Touch your students with your healing, soothing touch. Touch them, and they will know the touch of Christ.

Snubbed

Also a dispute arose among them as to which of them was considered to be greatest.

LUKE 22:24

She did it to me again. She's been doing it to me since we were in junior high school. She snubbed me. It wasn't one of those head-tossing, heel-turning snubbings. She's too subtle for that. It was a simple walk-by snubbing. I, with self-esteem fully intact, let that prepubescent feeling of insecurity take over my spirit again, if only for a split second. A little self-talk brought me back to reality. "OK, Linda, it is no less her problem now than it was thirty years ago. Move on."

Maybe there is a culture, a school, a church, or some conglomerate of people somewhere where snobbery does not exist—where there are no cliques, no educational, intellectual, or financial prerequisites, no judgmental dress codes, no fitness or body-shape requirements—but I can't think of one. The closest thing I can come up with is a nudist camp located about forty-five miles from my home, and I really don't want to go there. Besides, even they probably have a member who is snobbish about her flat abs and tiny waist, so they wouldn't qualify either.

While it seems as if I have been snubbed for almost every kind of deficit you could come up with, I have also been misperceived as a snob myself. A couple of summers ago, my friend Bekah and I were walking in a park in Seattle. We were wearing blue jeans and T-shirts, thinking we fit right in with the culture. A pair of young, hippie-like guys met us on the path and one of them said, "O-o-o, look at the rich ladies." We just looked at each other in disbelief. Unintentional walk-by snubbing.

I don't have a snobbish bone in my body—that is, until I come face to face with someone who does not meet my expectations in some way. Too big, too poor, too slow, too out of shape, too smelly, too showy, too haughty. My potential for snobbishness is vast.

Jesus had to warn his disciples against snobbery during his last meal with them. An argument had broken out among the disciples as to which one of them was considered to be the greatest. He who was indeed great reminded them that even he had come to serve. He took a towel and a basin, and while he washed their feet, he washed arrogance from their souls. He knelt in service to those who were contemplating their greatness. He showed them how much he loved them. They did not see their potential for pride and arrogance until Jesus served them.

Whether a given moment finds us the victim of our own or someone else's arrogance, Jesus calls us to serve. There is no room for snobbery in the lives of those who have been washed. Confronted by Jesus' love and servanthood, we humbly seek to serve others. Sometimes a simple smile can be our basin and towel. Give it a try—who knows what you will wash away.

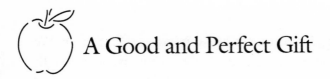

A Good and Perfect Gift

Every good and perfect gift is from above.

JAMES 1:17

In my bedroom hangs a quilt that was given to me by Bekah. Although my friend is a quilter, she didn't make this one. In fact, I was with her when she bought it, not knowing that eventually it would be mine.

During my growing up years, quilts in my family were purely functional. Both of my grandmothers had stacks of them made from fragments of cloth that were good for nothing else. I appreciated quilts for warmth but not for beauty, artistry, or meaning. As a child, I would recognize a scrap from a dress my grandmother had made but had no idea how much that scrap would come to mean later in life. Now I am careful not to use my quilts too often for warmth. They have become valued decorations and keepsakes in my house. My grandmothers' quilts seem ordinary to most who see them, but they are beautiful in my eyes. They were intended for an ordinary purpose, but now are a treasured gift.

On my birthday, I recognized the contents of the gift bag Bekah handed me as soon as I opened it. I spread the quilt out on the bed to admire and enjoy. A wide, blue geometric border surrounded six rectangles. Three of the rectangles contained pictures, and three had geometric designs. Something had been added, however. Within the frame of each picture, Bekah had embroidered a Scripture.

Beside the picture of a house was Joshua 24:15: "As for me and my house, we will serve the Lord." Above the shape of a pineapple, Galatians 5:22: "The fruit of the spirit is love, joy, peace." Over a silhouette of two children churning butter was Ephesians 5:21: "Submit to one another out of reverence to Christ."

I was overwhelmed. With the tender work of her hands, Bekah had changed a simple mosaic of cloth into an expression of friendship. With the tender work of her heart, she changes me. My home, my spiritual life, and my relationships, now illustrated and captioned, are influenced and strengthened by this valued relationship. The quilt hangs in private tribute to the fact that something ordinary can be made beautiful by the gentle work of relationship.

Each of us is both the giver and the receiver of such gifts, constantly changing others and being changed ourselves. Our lives flow in tribute. If the manner in which you influence lives today were to become a quilt hanging on a wall, would it be an ordinary ho-hum mosaic or a valued gift of beauty? May the work of our hands be fruitful and the good and perfect gift of our hearts be love.

 Moments

Command them to do good, to be rich in good deeds, and to be generous and willing to share. In this way they will lay up treasure for themselves as a firm foundation for the coming age, so that they may take hold of the life that is truly life.

1 TIMOTHY 6:18-19

"Would you hold for just a moment, please?" said the voice on the telephone.

"Sure," I replied, as if I could say no.

I was on the phone with a travel agent, making an airline reservation. We had exchanged some information when she asked me to hold for a moment. After about five minutes, she came back on the line and we exchanged a bit more information. Then, "Would you hold for just a moment, please?" What could I say?

"Sure," I said, exhaling the unspoken remains of my sentence. Her first "moment" had lasted five minutes, but this one stretched even longer. A moment is an undefined period of time, but clearly her perception of a moment and mine were not the same. To me a moment is a breath, even a glance, or it could be a memory, a period of time to be held in cupped hands. We live our lives in hours and days, months and years, but we remember them in moments.

Our lives can do a 180-degree turn in the matter of a moment. Life can change from a tunnel, with a limited focal point, to an expansive panorama in one simple moment. Our memories are filled with glimpses of life we know as moments. I remember the moment each of my sons made entrance into the world, the moment they each took their first step. There is a moment frozen in my memory of my grandfather feeding Jeff his first sweet potatoes at Thanksgiving dinner, a face-smeared, priceless moment.

I remember the moment my student Kacy "got it" with regrouping in multiplication. I remember the smile on Jonathan's face when he read, actually read, for the first time. I smile at the captured moment when Ben folded himself inside a cardboard box and jumped out just as I walked by. I laugh out loud at the moment when Steven sat on and then in the wastebasket.

My mind is overflowing with moments, some life changing, some fun, some eye-opening, some warm. Today will be no different than any other. It will be lived by the clock in hours and minutes. But today will contain treasured moments. Lock them in, for they will be tomorrow's memories.

Middles

I make known the end from the beginning.

ISAIAH 46:10

MIDDLES

I like beginnings and new things.
I like the beginning of a play,
   with overture and chattering crowd.
I like the cushy softness of new socks
   inside not so new shoes.
I like the beginning of a school year,
   with new notebooks full of waiting paper.
I like a new book whose resistant pages
   promise adventure.
Newness brings freshness and promise.

But I like middles, too.
Middles can be soft.
I remember being sandwiched in my grandmother's
   featherbed, with quilts piled up to my eyes.
Middles can be sweet,
Like that famous cookie middle we have been licensed to
   fiddle with.
Mostly, I think of middles as secure:
The middle of the night with ticking clock
   and quiet rhythmic breathing.
Middles are safe.

Our days are filled with beginnings and middles. The day itself has a beginning, and we can face it with glad expectancy or with only a hope of the mundane. But oh, the sweetness of those soft, secure middles. The relaxation of midday, the wisdom of midlife, and the pricelessness of friendships that began half a lifetime ago. I challenge you to count them today, your news and your mids, and to be thankful for each, exactly as it is.

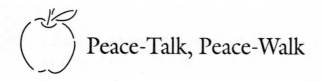

Peace-Talk, Peace-Walk

Blessed are the peacemakers, for they will be called sons of God.
MATTHEW 5:9

I remember the peace movement of the sixties. I remember sit-ins, love-ins, and whatever-ins, all "performed" in the name of peace. The "peacemakers" of the sixties were often long-haired, disheveled, and shoeless. Many of them sang songs and carried signs to demonstrate their desire for global peace. Some sat cross-legged, dropping acid and smoking grass, seeking inner peace, while their dark-suited government counterparts sat across tables from our national enemies and made peace-talk.

Jesus, the original long-haired, shoeless Peacemaker, made a lot of peace-talk, too. The angels sang "peace on earth" to announce his arrival upon this globe of greed and gravity. He is called the "Prince of Peace." He wanted us to be at peace with one another (Mark 9:50). He left peace, his peace, as a legacy for his followers (John 14:27). And he blessed the peacemakers among us, calling them children of God.

Who, then, are the peacemakers? Are they the singing, shoeless souls of the sixties? Are they the negotiators in three-piece suits? Are they the commanders of peace-keeping armies? No, we are the peacemakers, we who possess the peace of Christ.

One of Jesus' deepest desires for his followers was for unity. In John 17, he prayed to his Father in heaven "that they may be one as we are one." A peacemaker is one who brings about unity. The word "peacemaker" comes from several words meaning "connecting into one." A peacemaker is a catalyst for the connection of people to other people, and for the connection of people to their God. Blessed are you when you bring about connectedness rather than conflict, unity rather than alienation—for when you do this, you look a lot like your Father. There is a family resemblance. People will see that you are a child of God.

Unfortunately, we look more often like we belong to the Prince of Chaos than to the Prince of Peace. Our words bring division, our actions disconnect, and our judgments compromise the character of Christ. We promote our agenda and disguise our selfishness. We don't look much like our Father.

Peacemaking isn't always a cushy job, and it doesn't mean compromising truth. Just ask the Pharisees if Jesus was wishy-washy. He called a snake a snake and a coffin a coffin, never compromising who he was, never compromising the truth he came to reveal. He never compromised what he wanted for us, either: peace, his peace and unity. He spent his ministry teaching to that end.

What about you? Are you a peacemaker? Do you bring about connection and unity? If you do, you are blessed, and you look an awful lot like your Father.

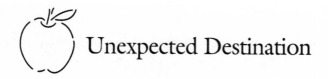 Unexpected Destination

But the plans of the Lord stand firm forever, the purposes of his heart through all generations.

PSALM 33:11

Imagine yourself preparing for a trip to Hawaii, the vacation of your dreams. You have been watching your diet for weeks, and you look great. You pack beach shoes, sunscreen, five rolls of film, evening wear, four swimsuits, and an extra pair of sunglasses. You are ready to go.

The day of departure finally arrives. The butterflies in your stomach could probably take you airborne. The flight is perfect, and you land on a pillow. This is it.

You step off the plane expecting to be welcomed by aloha's and leis, but there isn't a muumuu in sight. The skies aren't sunny, and the chilled air is nipping at your sleeveless arms. You see no souvenir-laden grandmas or flower-shirted, black-socked grandpas hurrying to catch their plane for home. People are going about their business in the airport terminal, but no one looks like a vacationer.

"This can't be right," you say to yourself. "Wherever this is, I'm not supposed to be here."

The only thing to do is to find the pilot who was responsible for bringing you here. "What's going on here?" you ask him. "I'm supposed to be in Hawaii."

"I know and I'm very sorry," he says. "We had to make an unexpected change of direction. You are not in Hawaii. You're in London."

"London! No wonder I'm freezing! When's the next plane to Hawaii?"

"There is no plane to Hawaii. I can't really explain it all now, but you simply won't be going."

"OK, then, take me back where I came from."

"I can't do that either. You are going to be here for awhile. You may as well adjust."

At one time or another, in one circumstance or another, we all have packed our bags for Hawaii and found ourselves instead in London. We have found ourselves in the midst of the unexpected. A sudden job change and relocation, the discovery of an unfaithful spouse, the death of a loved one, an unplanned pregnancy, a promotion, the birth of a handicapped child, all bring us to a place we never expected to be. Our circumstances can change in the blink of an eye.

The Bible is abundant with stories of people whose circumstances changed dramatically. Adam and Eve were relocated and given totally new job descriptions. Abraham and Sarah became new parents in their golden years. David, a shepherd, became king of Israel. Job, a wealthy and righteous man, lost everything he owned in one day. Jonah found himself living in some most unpleasant accommodations. Mary and Joseph became parents in a whirlwind of divine revelation. Fishermen became preachers following a carpenter-turned-rabbi.

It seems that almost no one had packed correctly for the coming destination. So often, neither have we. But the sovereign God of the universe knows your plans and he knows his plans. He knows about tomorrow today. God is never surprised. As you step from your plane onto unexpected ground, he will be there to greet you.

"You are going to be here awhile," he will say, "but I will be here, too."

71

 Never Give Up

[Love] always trusts, always hopes, always perseveres.

1 CORINTHIANS 13:7

I watched him go bouncing down the sidewalk, book bag shouldered and blond hair flying. He turned, smiled, and waved, "Good-bye, Mrs. Page. See you tomorrow!"

A mixture of emotions took me by surprise as I returned his parting gesture. Almost exactly a year ago I stood in the principal's office and wept as his parents took him away. They planned to check him into a treatment facility. His anger was unmanageable at home and at school. The best we could offer him hadn't worked.

He was away from school for six weeks of intense inpatient treatment. When he returned home, his parents dealt with endless weeks of outpatient follow-up, visits with psychologists and psychiatrists, new medication, and no medication. At school, he saw the crisis counselor; we wrote behavior plans. He responded; we praised. He resisted; we isolated. He fought; we restrained. We had good days, bad days, and really bad days. I would go home in the afternoon, tie on my running shoes, and try to take my body to the same level of crisis my soul felt. There was no leaving this problem at school.

Through it all, three things somehow brought sense to this labyrinth of emotion we all were walking through. There was prayer. I prayed, his classroom teacher prayed, the principal prayed, prayer groups prayed, my friends prayed, and I know this child's family prayed. We prayed at school, before school, after school, and through school. (So much for political correctness!) There was hope. Today was better than yesterday. This week was better than last week. So we had a setback. Tomorrow will be better. And there was trust. God cares.

Summer came, and so did a light at the end of the tunnel. One more doctor and one more therapist, a medication change, and the light grew brighter. School began, and so did yet another behavior plan. There were good days, bad days, and not so bad days. We began to see smiles, completed schoolwork, adjustment, and contentment. Then there were good days, not so good days, and really good days. Life offered a new perspective to us all.

Standing on the sidewalk that afternoon, I sensed the miraculous. God had given me a love for this child, a tenacious love that we teachers often reserve for those children for whom there seems to be little hope. Praise God for them: children who awaken a godliness in us that can come only as a gift from him—godliness that loves, trusts, hopes, and perseveres. Never give up. To God be the glory.

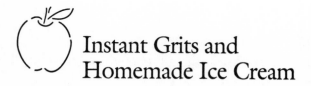

Instant Grits and Homemade Ice Cream

Wait for the Lord; be strong and take heart and wait for the Lord.
PSALM 27:14

I hate it. We all hate it, but we do it all day long. I start my day doing it as the coffee pot drips my source of wakefulness. I do it again in the car, honking reminders to whichever of my sons is running late. Stoplights make me do it on the way to school. I have to do it in the workroom at school because someone has beaten me to the copy machine. Probably my least favorite place to do it is on the phone, even when recorded music is playing in my ear. The longest I ever did it was for nine months. "It" is waiting.

Oh, how we hate to wait. In my pantry at this moment I have instant coffee, instant tea, instant oatmeal, instant soup, instant pudding, and instant grits. (Grandmother would roll over in her grave at the thought.) I don't have to wait to satisfy my thirst, my hunger, or my sweet tooth. The grocery store offers me an express lane, the bank has a "one transaction only" line, and the corner convenience store promises convenience to my schedule while greatly inconveniencing my budget. Oh, how we hate to wait, but is waiting really such a bad thing?

My grandparents had to wait on a lot of things that we have in the blink of an eye. They had to wait for the house to warm up on winter mornings, for breakfast to cook, and for the coffee to perk. They had to wait for the harvest to have fresh fruits and vegetables. They had to wait for the bread dough to rise, for the doctor to arrive, for the telephone line to be open. But with all of their waiting, there was time to be together while the cornbread finished baking, while the clerk gathered the grocery order together, while Grandmother squeezed a dozen lemons for a gallon of lemonade, while every cousin took a turn at the crank of the ice cream maker. Waiting was a treasure all its own.

Sometimes when I am out running errands with my best friend, I find myself troubled by a long line or a crowded store. "Relax," she will say to me. "We're together. Let's enjoy the wait." I forget all too easily to enjoy time given, to treasure the waiting.

I recently ran into a friend whose job was in limbo. He would know within a few weeks if he would stay or move on to something else. "I'm in the safest place I could be," he said to me. "Waiting on the Lord is such a safe place." He was treasuring the waiting.

With all of our instant this and microwave that, waiting continues to be a part of our lives. Sometimes we get to do it with our family, sometimes with a friend, sometimes we even get to do it with the Lord. Enjoy the gift and treasure the waiting.

Painful Awakenings

When I awake, I will be satisfied with seeing your likeness.

PSALM 17:15

- Indigestion had plagued him all day. He hadn't said much about it. He kept taking those little chewable tablets, but they hadn't helped very much. After a fourteen-hour workday, he was at last able to slip into bed beside his sleeping wife. A stabbing chest pain yanked him awake. As sweat popped out on his forehead, he was able to call his wife's name. Pain awakens.

- Her due date had passed last week. Bad timing seemed to be in control of everything, with her husband working the graveyard shift this week. Little Stevie, her two year old, had a nasty cold and hadn't slept well in a week. The last thing she remembered was putting her feet up on the coffee table to rest for just a minute. Her eyes flew open, and her thoughts raced. "What was that? Where am I? Is this it? ... Oh ... Yes, this is it!" Pain awakens.

- A teenage girl walked into the guidance counselor's office and closed the door behind her. Slumping into the overstuffed chair in front of the desk, her story spilled from a heart far too weary for her tender years. She was pregnant again. She had had two abortions already. None of the boys who had fathered her babies were anywhere to be found once they found out she was pregnant. Even her friends were accusing her of just looking for attention. Life for her had been a string of broken promises, from a mother's promise to go out for ice cream to a young boy's promise of eternal devotion. "I don't want to live this way anymore. Can you help me?" Pain awakens.

- A mother sat on her front porch steps. Her head fell between her knees as she began to sob in anguish. She had it all: beauty, influence, a handsome husband, three beautiful daughters, a home in the "right" neighborhood. A telephone call from school had sent her reeling. Her youngest daughter had been caught drinking at school. Her thoughts spun like a carousel out of control. Was this the opening of a Pandora's box? One secret would be out for sure. Her daughters were all in rebellion. Would the rest of their secrets come spilling out? Her marriage was loveless, her husband's drinking was becoming a problem, and in spite of outward appearance, their family was near financial ruin. "God, how could this happen to me? Help me, please!" Pain awakens.

Lord, awaken us now to twinges before the agony comes in full forever. Open our eyes to see your face and to seek your healing balm.

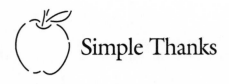 Simple Thanks

Give thanks in all circumstances, for this is God's will for you in Christ Jesus.

1 THESSALONIANS 5:18

I thought maybe it was a scene from wartime. On my television screen, I saw a line of children from an eastern country, each holding a bowl. They were in single file, moving toward a large steaming cauldron. The expectant child standing before the kettle would hand his bowl to the server. Placing his hands palm to palm, he would bow to the one serving him and gratefully accept his meal. Some of the children in line held bowls with rice already in them, but only if they brought the rice from home.

I was not watching a scene from a war-torn country. I was watching the school lunch program in progress in a school in Thailand. The steaming cauldron contained a brothy soup with a few vegetables. If a child was fortunate enough to bring some rice from home, he would have a nutritious and satisfying meal. If he brought no rice, he might well be hungry for much of the day. The commentary explained that the children do odd jobs and put on shows to earn money so that this soup can be served to them every day. No wonder they do not hesitate to bow in gratitude. They know the sting of hunger. They have learned the value of earning and the joy of reward.

Halfway around the world, children are standing in another line, but in their bacteria-killing soap-washed hands is a computer card, not a rice bowl. Their first stop is a computer terminal. The mechanical brain winks and beeps its approval as each card is inserted. The children walk, dance, or skip to a serving line. The rising steam before them comes not from a single soup pot but from a variety of items on today's menu. There are two meats, two vegetables, three kinds of milk, bread, fruit, and something for a sweet tooth. To the children in scene one it would be a banquet.

The line buzzes with chatter and wiggles from beginning to end. As lids are lifted from today's choices, there are moans and wrinkled noses.

"Gross!"

"We just had that last week."

"I'm not eating that stuff."

No bows. No folded hands. No acknowledgment that anyone has worked to buy, prepare, or serve this food. No gratitude to God the Provider for such abundance. None, that is, except from one little girl already seated at a table. In the middle of the revelry, she takes inventory of her meal, clasps her hands together, and bows her head. She is a Norman Rockwell painting in a gallery of abstracts, hope in the midst of confusion.

How can so many be so grateful for so little, while only one shows gratitude for so much? I wonder how long we can continue in such irony. I wonder how long we who have failed to express gratitude will continue in such plenty.

Listening Disability

It is better for you to enter life crippled than to have two feet and be thrown into hell.

MARK 9:45

Because I am a teacher, I am also a learner. The subject I seem to learn the most about as I am in relationship with my students is myself. Day after day as I teach, something happens that stimulates my thinking and helps me to know myself more.

My friend Bekah helped to bring this truth home yet again when she was working as a volunteer tutor in an adult literacy program. Her student was a thirty-one-year-old woman of color whose life had not included privilege and whose learning had not included reading. Annie wanted to learn to read because her daughter was about to start school. She wanted more than anything to be able to read bedtime stories to her little girl. Bekah shared this story of her first meeting with Annie.

"Bird," Bekah said as she pointed to the picture on the page.

"Bird," repeated Annie.

"Bird begins with what sound?"

"Buh," replied Annie with pride.

Next Bekah pointed to the picture of a cup, and Annie dutifully repeated the word.

"Cup begins with what sound?"

"Chuh," was her incorrect response.

"No, cup begins with the 'kuh' sound."

Bekah went on to the next picture, a girl. When asked for the beginning sound for the word "girl," Annie again responded, "Chuh."

And again, for the beginning sound of "hand," she hesitantly replied, "Chuh?"

Bekah sensed anxiety welling up in Annie, which probably hadn't surfaced since the last day she attended school. The analytical teacher-soul in Bekah began to consider the situation. "She knows all of the names of the letters of the alphabet, but she can't identify the sounds they make. Could it be that we are dealing with a disability? Could it be that she cannot connect a written shape with the sound it stands for in speech?"

Later as I thought about Bekah's experience with Annie's "disability" to perceive the sounds that letters make, I realized my own "disability" to perceive the "sounds" that come from the souls of my students. I know them all by name, but I do not always perceive their pain and heartache, the fears they have of going home, the dreams that they dream or dare not dream.

Sometimes my students are like the "ph" or the "ough" sounds. The way they look seems to be completely unconnected to the sound I think they should make. My "disability" is influenced by my expectations.

Only the Master Teacher can help me with my "disability." Lord, help me to see beyond their names and what they appear to be. Give me ears to hear the sounds of their souls. Teach me to blend sound and soul together so that I, too, may read and understand.

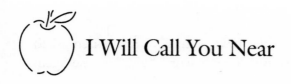

I Will Call You Near

Blessed are those who mourn, for they will be comforted.

MATTHEW 5:4

I usually thoroughly enjoy seeing the truth of Scripture lived out. But in one instance, I would not have chosen it to be so. December 2, 1995, began for me an abrupt and continuing experience of the second Beatitude, "Blessed are they that mourn...."

"Tell whoever it is that the boys are already asleep," my husband said as I answered the telephone. When the phone rings after 10:00 at night we assume it will be for one of our sons, but the voice on the line spoke to me.

"Linda, this is Pam. I have some really bad news." Her preparatory sentence gave my mind about one second to race through a thousand questions and to brace myself.

"What is it, Pam?"

"Cynthia Page has been killed."

Pam's voice seemed like it was a thousand miles away as I emotionally pulled back from news that was so hard to take in. Cynthia was the twenty-three-year-old daughter of my friend, but not relative, Lynn Page. Lynn's classroom is just one door down from mine, and we have been friends for almost twenty years. Cynthia had grown up before my eyes. She had graduated from college and was working at a restaurant, saving money to go to graduate school. She was bright, attractive, friendly, and had much to offer the world. Her life was taken from her, from all who knew and loved her, during a robbery.

Cynthia's death awakened questions and attitudes in me that I would have preferred not to meet. Why her? Why Lynn? Why, God? Where was your hand of protection? Why do I pray for protection for my own children? My friend is bearing unspeakable grief, and yet you say, "Blessed are those that mourn"?

Yet I watched as Lynn's faith rose like a phoenix from the fire. I saw her loving and comforting others. I observed as shoulder after shoulder came beneath her unbearable burden. I saw love abound and life overflow. I came to know that the answers to life's hard questions are not earthbound, and we insult our Creator's power in trying to make them so.

Mourning is an experience limited to this earthly life alone. In Matthew 5, Jesus promises us a heavenly connection during life's most incomprehensible circumstances. "Blessed are those that mourn," he says, "for they will be comforted." The word translated as "comforted" actually means "call near" in the original language. "When you mourn," he is saying, "I will call you near," a supreme, divine connection, a comprehensible truth. That promise was lived out before my very eyes.

Mourning is in your future and mine. To say that I now stand firm and unafraid would be far too bold and assuming, but I do know the truth of what I have seen. God makes good on his promises. Incomprehensible grief calls forth divine connection. "Blessed are those that mourn."

In memory of Cynthia Lynn Page:
June 10, 1972—December 2, 1995.

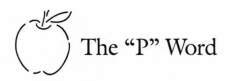

The "P" Word

But we also rejoice in our sufferings, because we know that suffering produces perseverance; perseverance, character; and character, hope.

ROMANS 5:3-4

Perseverance is a character quality that I deeply admire, but it is one that our instant, microwave, drive-through culture is valuing less and less. Perseverance requires, at its core, the other "p" word—patience. In evangelical circles, patience is spoken of as something to be feared, not sought. "Don't pray for patience," people say as though a ruthless God will zap you with some horrible circumstance just to show you.

I am really bothered that we steer away from patience and perseverance because I have seen those qualities in students who had little else going for them. Students have learned to read because they were willing to try again today what was so hard for them yesterday. Others have tried again and again to subtract with regrouping. What was there yesterday, sometimes seems erased from the memory bank.

I have seen in my neighborhood two examples of perseverance that shame the patience of most of us. When we first moved in, I noticed an elderly lady walking down her driveway. A silver cane glistened in her right hand. Her left arm dangled, palm out. She would jam the cane ahead of her, plant her right foot forward, and drag her left to meet it. This was no morning stroll; this was work. This was determination. I've watched this routine for three years now, day after day. I don't know if she prays for patience, but she has an ample supply.

A little farther down the street is another tenacious soul, a middle-school-aged boy. Because I know some of his teachers, I know that he has a brilliant mind, but due to a muscle disease, he has a most uncooperative body.

About a year ago he began a wobbling attempt to ride an old banana-seat bicycle. At first he could go only a few feet, with his front tire seeming to lead him all over the driveway. Start, stop, start, stop, again and again. After what seemed like weeks, he finally was able to make the trip from one end of his driveway to the other. I am sure it was a glorious day. Day after day, he worked. Now he rides wherever he wants to go in the neighborhood. He always wears a helmet, wisely protecting his greatest asset.

Somehow, I know that he will face all of life's challenges with the same spirit. Does he pray for patience? I don't know, but God has clearly given him the gift of perseverance.

If life held no challenges, we would need no perseverance. If there were no waiting, we would need no patience. Every life has some of both. Praying for patience does not bring crisis, nor does praying for perseverance bring heartache. Both are necessary for facing and triumphing over the crises and heartaches of life. Both are to be sought, as a precious treasure. Perseverance is worth the challenge, and patience is worth the wait!

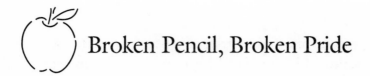 # Broken Pencil, Broken Pride

Unless you change and become like little children, you will never enter the kingdom of heaven.

MATTHEW 18:3

The morning went badly. To begin with, it had stormed all night. It had been one of those lightning-in-your-face, thunder-to-roll-you-out-of-bed kinds of nights. Crankiness prevailed in the school hallways. The power had been out, and you've never seen so many bad-hair days. There's nothing quite like bad hair to amplify a lousy mood. Thanks to the lack of power, I had had to cancel my Friday morning Bible study so I hadn't had my usual spiritual lift. But I had my act together. As the spiritual mentor of many, I planned to be Christlike today if it killed me.

I went to my mailbox and found a form that was a day late and only partially completed. "I can handle this," I thought to myself. "I will be kind. I will let no unwholesome words proceed out of my mouth. I will be an example of understanding."

The fifth grade was supposed to have gone on a field trip today. Yesterday, the fifth-graders that I teach had completed all of their work for the week. Now the field trip was canceled. "Great, now I have twelve special-education students with no plans and no work," I thought, "but I will have an attitude of gratitude."

I was keeping my head while all around me others were losing theirs. I scavenged some work for my fifth-graders and set to work with my fourth-graders. Lance and I were working in math when I noticed that he was using the stump of a pencil with no eraser. Aha! Another chance to be like Jesus. I would dig deep into my pocket and give this child a dime with which to go to the school bookstore and purchase a pencil. He would clearly see the love of Jesus in my eyes, so I mustered up the kindest expression I could create. "Lance, is that the only pencil you have?"

"Yes, Ma'am." As I thrust my hand into my pocket and drew a compassionate breath, he finished what he was saying. "You see, Miz Page, Will didn't have a pencil, so I broke mine in two and gave him half."

Nothing strikes so stunning a blow as my own arrogance. What was inhaled as compassion was breathed out in humility. While I was busy being every Christian cliché in the book, Lance was authentically being Christ to his classmate. Will received the compassion of Christ, but I felt his stinging rebuke. Through a simple act, a fourth-grade child had taught me a lesson I will never forget.

In my Bible, beside Matthew 18:3, you will find the name "Lance" in the margin.

 Itis and Ism

He who walks with the wise grows wise, but a companion of fools suffers harm.

PROVERBS 13:20

On Tuesday morning, Anna and Chip were absent from my class. Anna and Chip sit one behind the other in the second row. On Wednesday, Leigh was also absent. She sits in the fifth row, but she lives next door to Anna. By Thursday, seven students were on the absentee list, and on Friday the number was up to twelve.

A highly contagious viral gastritis was making its way through my class and the entire school. The incubation period of this virus was seventy-two hours, so by the time someone became sick, everyone he or she had come into contact with in the past three days had been exposed. Students and teachers were "dropping like flies." Even the principal fell prey to the illness. As usual, I was a die-hard observer of the epidemic.

Years of teaching have granted me a powerful immune system. Hardly a viral "itis" in the country can take what my white blood cells can dish out. I also wash my hands a lot and stay on the lookout for runny noses. I feel fairly safe from contagious "itis's" floating in the air, but I never let my guard down when an "ism" is near.

An "ism" can be even more contagious than an "itis." "Ism's" are people-borne rather than airborne. You may have come into contact with them as well. Negativism, legalism, racism, materialism, and you-name-it-ism can enter your classroom riding on the wings of a colleague's attitude. The next thing you know, that "ism" has entered your ears, walked through your brain, and flown right out of your mouth. With that, you become "ism-contagious," and soon your entire grade level or department is infected.

The best way to keep from becoming "ism-contagious" is to become "ism-conscious." Watch for symptoms. "Ism-bearers" rarely smile unless they have won an argument. They make fun of students and question the authority of administrators. They don't like the curriculum, the materials, the textbooks, or the snacks in the snack machine. Worst of all, they have the ability to make you agree with them even if, for example, you absolutely love the chocolate-covered peanuts dispersed from the snack machine. An "ism-attack" can leave your head spinning and your mouth babbling about things you don't even understand.

As surely as you wash your hands after you have been with a sneezy, drippy student, you have to clear your mind after an "ism-assault." Your convictions and your ability to think for yourself have only been temporarily sidetracked.

When you can, avoid "ism-contact." The Bible tells us to avoid the company of fools, and "fool" is just another name for an "ism-bearer." You can also build up your "ism-immunity" by staying in touch with your true self when an "ism-bearer" is around. When you stop agreeing with them, "ism-bearers" will eventually leave you alone.

We have much to watch out for, but we are strong. Isaiah 35:4 says, "Be strong, do not fear," and neither "itis" nor "ism" will overcome.

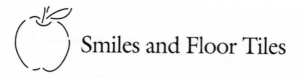

Smiles and Floor Tiles

The Lord does not look at the things man looks at. Man looks at the outward appearance, but the Lord looks at the heart.

1 SAMUEL 16:7

Lawrence knows every crack in the sidewalk from the driveway to the front door of his school. He knows that if he kicks away the grass in the big crack, it will be back by the next week. He knows where small chunks of tile are missing from the hall floor. He knows where Miss Elaine leaves the trash she has swept out of her room. He knows that it might rain today because the teacher assistant at the school entrance has her galoshes tucked behind the front door. He even knows that Mr. Hall, the principal, has a meeting today because he is wearing his wing tips and not his Hush Puppies. Lawrence knows all about floors and feet, because he doesn't look up at eyes and faces.

Lawrence has some learning problems, mixed with attention deficit disorder. The world can be, for him, a most confusing place. Left seems right, and right seems south. When he is reading, he sees the word "help" with his eyes, but his mouth says "play." His teacher tells him to pay attention, but he thinks, "To what?" Sometimes when he is confused he asks for help, but most people can't explain things so that he can understand. Floor tiles and shoelaces make a better point of reference for Lawrence than people do.

Lawrence's mother is his great encourager. Last year she would tell him every morning to look at the teacher assistant at the front door, smile at her, and say good morning.

"It will be great," she told him. "Start your day with a smile."

After many weeks of prodding, Lawrence found his courage one brisk winter morning. He stepped out of his mother's car, raised his chin from his chest, looked the nice lady in the eye, and smiled.

"Good morning," he said.

Nothing. She said nothing, did nothing, saw nothing.

"Maybe she had a bad morning," his mother told him the next day. "Try again."

And try he did, every morning for two weeks. Nothing. Absolutely nothing. Lawrence has since regained his expertise in floor tiles but lost his faith in smiles. His mother, Ally, penned this poem as Lawrence's plea.

PLEASE LOOK AT ME

Please, look at me,
If only for a moment.
Show me you care.
This moment will never happen again.

Please touch me,
A warm, gentle touch.
Show me you care.
A simple hug will do.

Please hear what I am saying.
It means so much
For you to understand.
I want to be understood.

Please spend this day looking, smiling, listening, and touching. It will change a life.

Maybe yours.

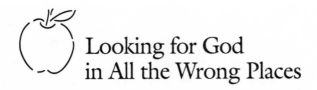 Looking for God
in All the Wrong Places

My eyes fail, looking for my God.

PSALM 69:3

Chip shot practice in the front yard is hardly a time when you would expect to find gold. My son, Jeff, was about to draw back his lob-wedge when something shining in the grass caught his eye. "Probably just a gum wrapper," he thought. The ball landed softly in our neighbor's front yard, but Jeff's eye was drawn back to the winking sparkle just ahead.

About a year before, the boys were playing football in the front yard with a large group of neighborhood kids. My husband, David, decided he would go outside, and I knew I wouldn't see him for a while. When I looked out the front window, sure enough, David was fading back to throw a pass. Smiling to myself, I went back to preparing supper.

About twenty minutes later my younger son, Michael, opened the front door and shouted, "Mom, come help us look. Dad has lost his ring."

Outside, opposing football teams had become a unified search party looking for David's gold nugget ring. Some of the kids were on their hands and knees, faces low and fingers raking. Others were fanned out where the game hadn't even been played, but searching just the same. A few were standing, nonchalantly dragging one foot through the grass, looking but trying to look uninterested. One or two had gone home. After all, the fun was over.

The search continued as long as the light allowed, but the lost treasure eluded us all. The next day, a friend went over the entire lawn with a metal detector. Two old bolts and a penny were all that he found. The ring seemed to have vaporized. We finally gave up the search and put the ring out of our minds—that is, until that sparkle caught Jeff's eye more than a year later.

Jeff took a swipe with his golf club at the object embedded in the dirt. One man-sized, mud-covered, gold nugget ring rolled onto the grass. Jeff had done what no one else had: he looked in the right place. It seemed that none of us armed with filtering fingers or metal detector had actually been to the spot where the ring lay.

How like our search for God was this little treasure hunt in my front yard. Some of us do a hands-and-knees search, looking closely where we think God might be. We deeply search every self-help and mind/body/soul technique known to man. Others search, but only where convenience leads. Some of us halfheartedly test the waters but don't want anyone to know what we are up to. Then there are those who choose not to look at all. Searching for God just doesn't sound like much fun.

Like the ring, God is where he is. He reveals himself to us from there. God has proved himself in creation and revealed himself in his Word and his Son. The search for God is not so hard; all we have to do is look where he is.

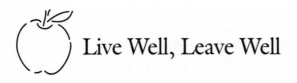 # Live Well, Leave Well

Her children arise and call her blessed.

PROVERBS 31:28

I recently took my boys to the doctor for physicals. Considerable gloating took place at the weighing and measuring station. They are both now taller than I am, not to mention stronger and faster. My younger son, Michael, is only an inch and a half shorter than Jeff, who is two years older. My guess is that next year Michael will have even more bragging rights.

What a bittersweet gift are these two strong, healthy boys! To think they began life as a tiny speck inside my womb. They grew and kicked and tumbled their way into the world and wailed at the sight of it. Their comfort then was to snuggle next to the heartbeat they had heard during those warm, dark months. But little by little, they each began to explore their world with eyes, hands, mouth, and feet. They crawled, they walked, they spoke, they ran. And so their leaving began. Bittersweet, indeed, to watch with pride as they grow, and heartache as they leave.

I am reminded that nothing I do and no time I spend is more important than doing and being with these two. I spend my days teaching, caring for, and loving other people's children. I am convinced that there is no profession in the world more powerful or valuable than the teaching profession. However, no matter how important my paying job may be, the job at home is even more important. Somehow after working and giving all day, I need to have some of the best of me left for after 3:30 in the afternoon. The two youngsters who live at my house need my love and attention in a far deeper way than anyone who takes a seat in my classroom. Balancing the giving of myself is often the hardest choice of my day.

Statistics show us that fewer and fewer moms are choosing to stay at home. No one understands the choice to work better than I do, but I salute the stay-at-home mom. With new research showing the importance of the first three years of development, stay-at-home moms are at last being seen as valuable, not only to their children but to the future of society. I impact society by nurturing and guiding my two teenaged boys as well. Dr. Bernadine Healey says that for children, the most important brain food is parental love and attention. Perhaps it will have an equally healing effect on our world.

Each time my boys walk out the door, I think of how short my time with them is becoming. I am compelled to ask myself if I have given them the best of myself each day. I am striving to answer that question with yes more often than no, to savor the sweetness of having them with me. Their leaving is in progress. They need the best of me to live well and the best of me to leave well.

Divine Designer Wardrobe

For all of you who were baptized into Christ have clothed yourselves with Christ.

GALATIANS 3:27

I just spent an afternoon shopping for a jacket to wear for a photograph. I really hate shopping, probably because when it comes to clothing, I have excessive expectations. On this particular shopping trip, I was looking for a jacket that conveyed who I am and, at the same time, made me look thin—which I am not. I wanted something that would hide my every vulnerability and still project an aura of wisdom. I wanted something that looked young and snappy, even though I am a few years past Generation X and more snapped than snappy. I wanted a jacket that slenderized, deemphasized, and intellectualized. As I said, I have very high expectations.

Jesus told us not to worry about what we wear. Even in his culture, certain garments had certain significance. Tassels, quality, and color all served as outer proclamations of the inner man. There is nothing new under the sun. Street gangs identify themselves by style, color, and name brand, but then don't we all? Clothing is our silent way of showing who we are, who we think we are, and who we wish we could be. Preachers wear collars, businessmen wear starched shirts, golfers wear a variety of animals and crests on their shirts. The rich don original designer dresses, and the not-so-rich break their budgets in imitation. I stand dizzy in the center of a shopping mall and wonder what Jesus would say about millions of square feet of merchandise that he hoped would be insignificant. We have given such power to thread and cloth.

Clothing stands as a shield between vulnerability and exposure. Adam and Eve had no wardrobe worries in the Garden, but discovered their exposure as soon as they ate the forbidden fruit. Suddenly they were afraid to be seen and known. A new sensation overtook Adam. He called it shame. As fallen humanity, their first act was to make clothes for themselves. Adam and Eve tried to cover their shame with leaves. God intruded upon their shame with grace.

In our world, shame is often covered by garments that show power, prestige, position, or rebellion. Much as with our ancient parents, beneath these coverings beat hearts that are racked with fear and shame. Those very hearts walk into our lives every school day when our students enter our classrooms. The clothing they choose is an attempt to keep them safe from intrusion by a world they do not wish to join. We can choose to be fashion critics, or we can choose to be grace intruders.

Our divine Designer tells us to clothe ourselves with humility, righteousness, and compassion. With such fashion statements as these available, no wonder he told us not to worry about clothing. No wonder he calls us to follow his lead, clothing ourselves with character that moves us toward those with hidden, fearful, and shame-filled hearts.

 The Story Is Mine

Were not our hearts burning within us while he talked with us on the road and opened the Scriptures to us?

LUKE 24:32

I have been reading the Bible with varying degrees of interest as long as I can remember. As a child, I read more Bible "stories" than actual text. There was the story of Adam and Eve, the story of Moses and the Hebrew people, the story of Noah, the story of King David, and of countless other Old Testament characters. The stories didn't stop with the Old Testament. I remember the story of Jesus' birth, the story of the woman at the well, the Good Samaritan, the Prodigal Son, stories told and stories lived, lessons learned and lessons lived.

When we read stories, detachment is easy. We can point an accusing finger at the evils of a wicked stepmother and know she is everything that we will never be. We can read of Abraham Lincoln without feeling compelled to find something of ourselves in John Wilkes Booth. We can even read a self-help book and find all of the ways it could improve our spouse or next-door neighbor. We can weep at a tragic ending but lay the tragedy on the bedside table. Not so as we read the Word of God.

As I see the reality contained within the truth, I find that the Bible is in fact not only a true story; it is my story. It tells my own story as one who has been created by a holy God, as one who has seen, smelled, grasped, and tasted the fruit of temptation, finding it sweet in the mouth but bitter to the soul.

It is the story of people like me whose hearts grow cold, while standing beside the flame of miracles. It is the story of one who sometimes has the faith and perseverance to construct an ark of truth and who sometimes must cry out, "Help my unbelief!" It is the story of someone who awakens in a foreign land and longs for the warmth of home. It is the story of someone whose grave clothes have been removed, a new creation for whom the stench of death is forever held at bay. It is the story of someone who is forgiven much and who desires to love much. It is the story of one who desires to sit at the feet of the Master and who does so while others scurry about in frustration. It is the story of one who realizes down the road of healing that he forgot to say "thank you." It is a story that I deeply want to understand.

Where will I find myself today as I open the Word? The story is mine. It has a victorious conclusion. The story goes on....

 Licey Lucy

Daughter, your faith has healed you.

Lucy had to be sent home from school for the third time this semester. The school nurse confirmed that, once again, Lucy was infested with head lice. She waited alone in the sickroom, sitting cross-legged on the bed with the plastic-covered mattress. In the next room, the office staff went about business as usual, scratching their heads a bit more often than seemed necessary.

Lucy knew the routine well. The teacher would send her to the nurse. The nurse would snap on a pair of disposable gloves and proceed to dig around in Lucy's hair. "There they are," she would say. "Better call her mom." One of the secretaries would then call Lucy's mother. Sometimes Mom came right away. Sometimes Lucy would spend the whole day in the sickroom, waiting. No one knew quite what to do with Lucy.

Lucy couldn't help the fact that lice took up residence in her hair. Lucy's house, furniture, and bed were lice-infested. Lucy was called "Licey Lucy" by some of the students. She was an "untouchable." Nobody wanted to be near her.

Jesus had an encounter with a sort of "Licey Lucy." The fifth chapter of Mark tells us of a woman "who had been subject to bleeding for twelve years." She had spent all of her money seeing doctor after doctor, but instead of getting better, she had gotten worse. According to the Torah, she was also considered impure. Every bed on which she lay was a bed of impurity. Everything on which she sat was considered unclean, and any person she touched would be made unclean. She was an untouchable, a "Licey Lucy."

Jesus was in town and was being followed by great crowds of people. The woman moved shoulder-to-shoulder in the crowd. If someone recognized her, she would be run out of town. Tradition would not allow a woman to touch a man's garment unless he was a member of her family.* Maybe she thought breaking tradition would be better than breaking the Law of Torah. She would just try to touch Jesus' clothes.

When she was close enough, the woman did something she had not done in twelve years. She reached out her hand to another human being. Instantly upon touching Jesus' garment, she was healed. Instantly Jesus knew someone had touched him.

"Who touched me?" he asked, looking around. Terrified, the woman fell at Jesus' feet and told him what she had done. Jesus responded to her in the one way that made her action acceptable. He made her a part of his family. "Daughter," he said, "your faith has healed you."

What would Jesus do with "Licey Lucy"? He would treat her like family. Unlike Jesus, you and I can't heal her with a simple touch ... or can we?

*Charles R. Page II, *Jesus and the Land* (Nashville: Abingdon, 1995), 91-94.

 Shine

Your word is a lamp to my feet and a light for my path.

PSALM 119:105

My grandparents lived so far out in the country that, once the lights in the house were turned off at night, no lights from nearby towns, farms, or roads could be seen. I remember spending the night with my grandparents as a child and straining in the darkness to see my hand in front of my face. Determination had no effect on the outcome. My grandmother called this absolute darkness "midnight under a skillet."

The deepest darkness I have ever experienced was purposely demonstrated during a tour of Mammoth Cave in Kentucky. All of the tours are safe and well lighted, but when the tour group is in the largest underground room on the tour, the guide throws a master switch, turning out every light.

I remember reaching for the hands of my young sons as the guide warned us of what he was about to do. I'm not sure if I took their hands for their security or mine, but when the lights went out I was glad to be connected to my children. Even the assurance that the lights would soon be turned back on did not keep my heart from beating a little faster.

The darkness under the earth is an engulfing, surrounding presence. It almost seems to have substance. It is inescapable and permanent. There is no skylight in the next room to penetrate this darkness, and no sunrise will erase it.

Shrouded by the blackness of Mammoth Cave, I grasped a new understanding of my need for light. Living in darkness would be a crouching, crawling, fearful existence. The only thing that is easy to do in darkness is to hide. As we waited helplessly in the gigantic cave, the tour guide struck a match. Suddenly, by the light of only a single match, I could see my children's faces. I could find the pathway that had brought us there and, even more importantly, the one that would lead us out.

Light is the enemy of darkness. With the entrance of light, feet immobilized by uncertainty can step forward with assurance. Crouching and crawling are no longer necessary. No matter how large the sphere of darkness or how small the flicker of light, the darkness cannot engulf the light, but light actually negates the existence of darkness.

Jesus said, "I am the light of the world," and in entrusting his light to his followers, he commissioned them to let their light shine before others. As we live in a world of darkness, toil in workplaces of darkness, and live in neighborhoods that seem engulfed in darkness, we are called to shine. Darkness has been shattered. It doesn't have a chance.

Cody's Connection

Accept one another, then, just as Christ accepted you, in order to bring praise to God.

ROMANS 15:7

I first met Cody when he was in kindergarten. His teacher met me in the hall one day and asked me to come to her room to observe a student about whom she had some concerns. During my first visit at "story time," when the other children were seated on the carpet at the teacher's feet, Cody was belly-crawling through the maze of his classmates. Nap time was nonexistent for Cody, so he was allowed to wander around the room while the others slept, if he would do so quietly. Instruction time found Cody either at his teacher's side with her arm wrapped firmly around him or seated at his place doing something other than what he was supposed to do. In the end our assessments showed that he had more disabilities than we had originally imagined and that he unquestionably qualified as one of my special-education students.

Cody did not like change or intrusion in his life. School had brought both. He was introduced to a mile-long list of teachers and staff and more children than his little mind could contain. As we approached his first-grade year, the decision was made to bring in a personal assistant for him. Enter Peggy West, Cody's helper, advocate, defender, surrogate mom, and friend.

Peggy made the connection with Cody in the only way it

could be done, with subtlety and softness. She didn't overwhelm Cody; she just helped him. Peggy communicated to Cody that he was special, but never that he was different; that she expected him to work hard, but that he was not alone. Cody said little with words, but everything by his actions. Intrusions into his world were still unwelcome but no longer feared, as long as Mrs. West was near. I have often seen him rivet his eyes upon a perceived intruder as he reached for the security of Peggy's touch.

Through all of the hours of reading, math, auditory training, science projects, vocabulary tests, spelling tests, and a zillion other "school things," Cody moved to more and more independence. He began to talk more (much more), laugh more, interact more, and, at Peggy's urging, he completed more and more work. She pushed and he worked. She encouraged and he responded. She insisted and he amazed us. In so many ways through the years, Cody developed into a regular kid in a baggy shirt, running errands for his beloved "Mus Wes."

Relinquishing Cody to middle school was one of the hardest separations of my teaching career. Our need to be with him, to have daily input into his life, lost out to his need to move on, to grow up. The story of Cody and Peggy gives testimony to the power of connection. For Cody as a kindergartner, connection and security were missing. With Peggy's help Cody was able to find exactly what he needed. What a difference connecting can make!

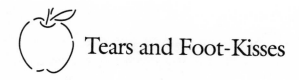 Tears and Foot-Kisses

Her many sins have been forgiven—for she loved much. But he who has been forgiven little loves little.

LUKE 7:47

Jesus must have been an incredibly interesting dinner guest. Perhaps that is why a certain Pharisee named Simon invited Jesus to his home, just to "pick his brain" or to hear what he would say. During dinner Jesus had an unusual encounter with a woman known by reputation as a "sinful woman." Since Jesus was reclining, his feet were extended behind him as he rested on his left elbow. The woman who appeared on the scene, and stood behind Jesus, was weeping. She was not sniveling; she was weeping, so much so that her tears began to wet Jesus' feet. She then knelt down and wiped Jesus' tear-soaked feet with her hair, pouring perfume on them and kissing them repeatedly.

Jesus' host was appalled. Knowing the woman's reputation caused him to question that of Jesus. He thought that if Jesus were a prophet, he would know about this woman and not allow himself to be defiled by her touch. Jesus read Simon's thoughts, however, which should have told Simon something about Jesus' status as a prophet. He responded to Simon's doubts by telling a story.

One man owed a moneylender fifty *denarii;* another owed five hundred *denarii.* Neither man had the money to pay back his loan, so the moneylender canceled both debts. Jesus' question to his host was, "Which of them will love (the moneylender) more?" Simon answered correctly by saying the one who owed the most would love the most.

Jesus then helped Simon find himself in the story. He pointed out to Simon that he had omitted several basic acts of hospitality when Jesus had arrived as a guest in his home. Simon had not offered to wash Jesus' feet, greeted Jesus with a kiss, or poured oil on his head. Simon had skipped all basic hospitalities, but the sinful woman had carried them out and more.

Jesus then drew an important connection between the understanding of one's forgiven-ness and the capacity to love: "Her many sins have been forgiven—for she loved much. But he who has been forgiven little loves little." The sinful woman expressed her love in a mighty way, for she understood her need for forgiveness. The Pharisee expressed his lack of love just as clearly. He stood in judgment of the intruding woman and offered only passing civility to Jesus.

What about us? Do we shout, "Thief!" by the way we treat a student who has been caught stealing? Or do we understand our own capacity for greed and materialism? Do we show repulsion at the one who has a reputation as a drug dealer? Or do we really see our own foolish ways of seeking satisfaction? What about the teacher who "bats her eyes" at a male principal? Do we make her the hot gossip topic, or do we know the lengths to which we ourselves will go for a little attention?

Maybe we have graded ourselves on the curve too long. Maybe we need to understand that we have all been forgiven much. Then, and only then, will we, like the sinful woman, be able to love much.

 Closet Pray-ers

Where two or three come together in my name, there am I with them.

MATTHEW 18:20

I can only imagine what he must have thought at first. Our principal unlocked the storage closet in the office as usual about half an hour before school was to begin. I am sure he was expecting to find paper clips, cellophane tape, copy paper, and ink pens. Much to his surprise, he also found five of his teachers circled together in the unlighted, tiny, four-by-six-foot room. The column of light that entered with him spotlighted my face. I opened my mouth to say something, I don't know what, while he seemed to take a quick inventory of who was present. A knowing smile spread across his face as he said, "Excuse me, ladies."

Kim was the first to start snickering as the door gently came to a close. "I think we're caught," she said as laughter completely overtook us all in the blackness of the dark closet.

"I wonder if he thinks we're in the black market paper clip business," Sandy said, trying to catch her breath.

"I can see the headlines now," added Leigh. "TEACHERS CAUGHT IN CLOSET, SMUGGLING UNDETERMINED NUMBER OF POST-IT NOTES."

"Do you suppose he really knows what we're doing in here, or do you think he's afraid to find out?" asked Jan between gasps for breath.

Actually, we were being very scriptural. The Bible tells us to "go into your closet, close the door, and pray" (Mt 6:6). We did exactly that; we just forgot that the principal had a key to our closet.

The rattling of Mr. Pearson's keys in the door brought comic relief to what had been a very serious moment. A marriage was in deep trouble, and five friends had gathered together before the start of the school day to pray. We may have caught our principal off guard, but he knew exactly what we were doing.

There are many advantages to having a principal who is a believer and a leader in his church. Not all public schools have a man of prayer at the helm. There are even greater advantages to being surrounded by a family of believers where you work. With a little creativity, a call to prayer can be arranged on any day.

Jesus promised us that where two or three come together in his name, he would be there as well. He made no requirements as to where you have to be or how you are to position yourself. He just promised to be there.

Jesus himself was in the supply closet with us that day. He heard the unity of our hearts as we pleaded with him for the healing of a marriage. He saw the tears roll down our faces. He felt the urgency of our request.

I don't think he fled when Mr. Pearson opened the door. I believe that he wrapped loving arms around all five of us and threw his head back in laughter. As we were enjoying each other, he was enjoying us. He poured his presence over us as we parted company to begin our day. He made good on his promise once again.

Good Gifts

If you, then, though you are evil, know how to give good gifts to your children, how much more will your Father in heaven give good gifts to those who ask him!

MATTHEW 7:11

Most of us have one—a dresser drawer, a closet shelf, a box hidden away. It's not a hiding place. It's a keeping place. Mine probably looks like every other elementary teacher's keeping place, filled with trinkets that hold meaning only to me. Each gift awakens a memory. Each memory rekindles a prayer.

In my keeping place is a "gold" bracelet that isn't so gold anymore. I find at least a dozen holiday pins winking their red, green, and diamond eyes as though waking up from a long nap. There are apple-shaped key rings designed especially for teachers, heart-shaped pins for Valentine's Day, and little velvet roses. A tiny stuffed puppy, whose occasion I cannot remember but whose giver comes easily to mind, stands guard inside my treasure chest of memories.

Many of my teacher gifts never make it to my box. I have eaten a mountain of cookies made for 4-H projects and an equal number of birthday cupcakes. My everyday life is filled with reminders that my students have given me. A tiny crystal cross, given to me by Josh, sits on my dresser, never letting me forget how precious every day is. When my house smells like peaches, the aroma comes from a simmer pot from Jeff, given at Christmas a decade ago. I have a whole collection of hand-painted jewelry from Stewart, whose mom is an artist. And, oh, the coffee mugs. I love my coffee mugs.

I remember outreaching arms and ear-to-ear grins that could not wait until time for the Christmas party.

"Open it now, Mrs. Page. Open it now!"

And there were the mysterious gifts that magically appeared on my desk. Across the room, a pair of eyes would say, "I hope she likes it."

Never has a student given me a gift they did not think was the best they could offer. Maybe that is what the Scripture means when it says "good gifts."

"Good gifts" must mean the best that can be offered, the best that can be found. Sometimes the Bible speaks in absurdities. Matthew 7:9-10 suggests the absurdity of giving something harmful to one that you love. "Which of you, if his son asks for bread, will give him a stone? Or if he asks for a fish, will give him a snake?" We offer to those we love gifts that nourish and bring joy.

At the same time, those who love us want to give us the very best. They bring us good gifts. I have a box full and a heart full. I have an opportunity to give of myself today. How can I give anything less than my best? Today, I will give good gifts.

 # Begin Again

Create in me a pure heart, O God, and renew a steadfast spirit within me.

PSALM 51:10

I am a runner. Well, a jogger and a trotter, maybe? OK, I move forward at a pace a little faster than a walk ... most of the time. I hit the road most days with Bekah, a tall, thin blonde who could literally run circles around me, but thankfully does not.

I yearn for the days when a 10-K left me refreshed and energized. Those days are long gone. I am satisfied with much lower ambitions now, but even those often go unmet. It seems that I just keep having to start over. A back injury, a bad hip, a minor surgery. I am repeatedly on the comeback trail, repeatedly returning to square one.

Square one is not my favorite place to be in anything. I have noticed that no one ever begins a new project by saying, "Let's go to square one." Square one is always a place to be visited when something has gone wrong, didn't fit, or fell flat. "Back to square one," we say—and usually not with enthusiasm.

As I stand on square one, however, I find that I am in sacred company. Gerald Mann says that the underlying theme throughout Scripture is "new beginnings," a return to square one.

Adam and Eve underwent probably the most famous new beginning in all of history. After the fall, God changed the game plan and relocated them, but they were given a fresh start. God told Abraham to go to a new land for his new beginning. Psalm 51 is a plea to God from David, king of Israel, for a chance to begin again. Over and over, God wipes the slate clean and invites his people to square one. Jesus did the same, issuing an invitation to square one, wrapped in forgiveness.

"Neither do I condemn you," he told the woman caught in adultery. "Go and sin no more."

"Lovest thou me, Peter?" he said to his sometimes difficult disciple. "Feed my sheep."

When I go wrong, don't fit, or fall flat, I am not condemned to stay where I am. The Forgiver of my soul knows no limit to his forgiveness. He forgives, and I start fresh. I arrive at square one, and I have been changed. I am forgiven, and I am wiser.

So, I double knot my running shoes one more time and take my position on square one. I shake off my sense of failure, my shame. Shame will weigh me down. Shame has no place on square one.

I will be breathless, red-faced, and tired at first. Every hill will seem a mountain, but with my new wisdom will come new strength. I look beside me and there stands the Encourager of my soul, ready to take every step with me. I will start again. It will not be easy, but I am in fine company.

The Good News Is ...

A cheerful look brings joy to the heart, and good news gives health to the bones.

PROVERBS 15:30

Sometimes my husband will finish a phone conversation, hang up the phone, and look at me over the top of his glasses. "Well," he will say, "I have some good news and some bad news. Which do you want first?"

I always ask for the bad news. Take the pill first, then the sugar coating. I hope you have the same preference. I have good news and bad news, so I'm going to give you the bad news first.

The bad news is that the world is a mess. Crime is astronomical. Our inner cities are centers of drug trafficking and abuse. Gangs and gang violence are in control of neighborhoods and are becoming surrogate parents to our children. Murder has become the method of choice to control others and demonstrate power. Our children are becoming children of fear. All over America, "role models" are teaching young people that the goal of life is to do what you want when you want to, and to hold such control over others that no one would dare to get in your way.

Young people are having sex at younger and younger ages. Student pregnancy and sexually transmitted diseases have made their way into elementary schools. Youngsters are choosing forms of entertainment that involve graphic sex, graphic violence, and filthy language.

Throughout the country, youngsters have a smorgasbord of hatred from which to choose. They can choose to hate those of another gang, another race, another religion, another country, or they can just choose hatred as a way of life, period. The weapons of hate are readily available, bringing with them feelings of power and control.

The bad news goes on. It multiplies and it reproduces. The bad news comes to school, sits in your classroom, and goes right on being bad news right before your eyes. What is the good news? How can there even be any good news? The good news is ... you.

In the midst of all of the bad news, you, the image-bearer of Christ, are the good news. You walk the hallways of your school enveloped by the good news of the gospel, the news that the bad news in you has been redeemed. You teach differently, you see the world differently, you love differently.

Every day you penetrate the bad news with who you are. Every day students and teachers alike walk away after being with you, feeling valued and encouraged. Students talk about your fairness, and teachers find you easy to work with. You are the image-bearer of Christ, the Master Teacher. There is no doubt, the bad news is really bad, but the good news is, oh, so good!

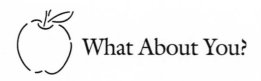 What About You?

You do not want to leave too, do you?

JOHN 6:67

The last few weeks had been pretty rough on Jesus. His healing ministry was in full swing, and his reputation as a healer was spreading. Besides, healing had brought a little girl back from the dead. He had cast so many demons out of a Gentile man that it took a whole herd of pigs to hold them all.

The miracle that brought him the most attention, and consequently the most trouble, however, was when he took a little boy's lunch and turned it into a sit-down dinner for over five thousand people. After that, the people decided that it was time to turn this rabbi into a politician. What he could do with a couple of fish and some barley loaves was unbelievable! They needed a man like this for a king.

Jesus knew they needed a little cooling-off period, so he and the disciples headed back to Capernaum. The disciples made the trip by boat. Jesus went part of the way on foot and the rest of the way by boat at warp speed.

The people who had attended Jesus' spur-of-the-moment banquet wanted more, so they followed Jesus to Capernaum. The Teacher decided it was time to give his class the big comprehension test, to see who could move to the head of the class (a first-century test for the gifted program). "I tell you the truth," he said, "you are looking for me, not because you saw miraculous signs but because you ate the loaves and had your fill" (Jn 6:26). Jesus knew exactly what had motivated his students.

Next, he gave them the big picture, the main idea: "I am the bread that came down from heaven" (Jn 6:41). Some religious leaders were in the crowd. They began to ask each other, "Isn't this Joseph and Mary's son?" (which was another way of saying, "Who does he think he is?").

Jesus then followed up the main idea with supporting details. "I am the living bread that came down from heaven. If anyone eats of this bread, he will live forever. This bread is my flesh, which I will give for the life of the world" (Jn 6:51).

With that he had the class arguing among themselves. "How can he give us his flesh to eat?"

Time for the final point. "Whoever eats my flesh and drinks my blood remains in me, and I in him" (Jn 6:56).

With that, many of his followers decided that Jesus' teaching was just too hard to accept. They turned and walked away. They dropped out of school. Jesus turned to the twelve disciples, who were probably sitting together, and administered the final exam: "You do not want to leave too, do you?"

In today's world, Jesus is said to have been One who lived in both the physical and the spiritual world. Many follow the teachings of Jesus that make them comfortable, the "feel good" gospel. But when it comes to sacrifice, the shedding of blood, atonement for sin, and other unpleasantries, the teaching becomes too controversial. When it comes to unpopular choices, many would-be disciples become dropouts.

What about you and me? Jesus' question remains the same. May we, as Peter did, pass the final exam with flying colors. "Lord, to whom shall we go? You have the words of eternal life."

White Knuckle Ride

Put [your] hope in God, who richly provides us with everything for our enjoyment.

1 TIMOTHY 6:17

"Enjoy the ride!" the attendant said to me as he checked my safety harness.

"Cute," I thought. "Really cute. I'll ride, but don't expect me to enjoy this."

Roller coaster rides have never been what I consider enjoyable. It just didn't make sense to me to stand in line for an hour in order to spend three minutes in misery. Seeing people exiting a roller coaster laughing and reliving the moment only served to convince me that they were nuts. But on this one occasion, the potential for ridicule by the middle schoolers I was chaperoning was just too much to bear. So there I was, strapped into the lead car that promised to whisk me, against my will, in every direction including upside down.

The initial hill climb was forty-five seconds of torturous anticipation. We crested the hill and dipped into a blur of roar and speed. I was certain that only the outer shell of my body was descending. My soul, my spirit, and my insides remained at the top of the hill, a sort of out-of-body experience. We jerked left and yanked right. We dipped. We swerved. We dangled upside down. Suddenly, without warning, we lurched forward and began to crawl up yet another hill of impending doom.

I noticed something interesting on this second climb. I seemed to be the only white-knuckled passenger on this train. Everyone else was laughing, whooping, and high-fiving. "They're all too young to have sense enough to be scared," I decided in my own defense, but a quick assessment of the patrons let me know that I was incorrect. I was by no means the oldest passenger. I was just the only one who wasn't enjoying the ride.

Halfway up the second ascent, I experienced an attitude-changing moment. With the motivation of saving face, I had been stubbornly determined to simply endure this agonizing experience, denying myself the freedom to consider that the ride just might be fun. I began to realize that, like so many of life's experiences, this one had a 100-percent survival rate and a gigantic potential to make me smile.

Drawing a life-giving breath, I released my death grip on the safety bar and left my stubbornness at the top of hill two. What a difference! Down we flew! We still yanked, jerked, and swerved. But this time I felt the wind in my hair and the G-force on my face. From deep inside, a laugh was born that flew right out of my mouth, joining forces with the squeals and shrieks of my fellow passengers. As we rolled to a stop, I heard myself having fun, a pleasant punctuation to a hilltop decision.

So often I approach life as I did that roller coaster ride, determined to get from point A to point B, but equally determined not to enjoy it. God has given me gifts to enjoy, not just to get the job done. My family and friends, my writing and speaking, my teaching job, my students, even my jeep with the top down, are all gifts for my delight.

Lord, help me to release my white-knuckled determination. Help me to find the wind in my hair, to give birth to laughter. Help me to enjoy the ride.

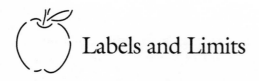 Labels and Limits

Anyone who says to his brother, "Raca," is answerable to the Sanhedrin. But anyone who says, "You fool!" will be in danger of the fire of hell.

MATTHEW 5:22

The school secretary called me on the "squawk box" one day to let me know I needed to stop by the office to review the file of an incoming student. Whenever a permanent record arrives, I look through it to see if there is any indication of a need for special services. I detected an urgency in the secretary's voice, so I made my way to the office as soon as possible. When I saw the inch-thick folder, I understood why she was eager for me to come by.

As I thumbed through Katy's record, my brain began to associate certain words and abbreviations with the yet-unseen child. Special education, ADD, LD, TBS, OT, PT—paper after paper certified a variety of handicapping conditions and services needed. I found myself forming opinions and making judgments about Katy before we ever met. She may as well have walked through the door with all of the labels I had given her tattooed on her forehead. Thankfully she did not. Though the issues and needs shown in Katy's record were correct, my preformed opinion was not.

I met Katy the day after I had read her file. She was a beautiful eleven-year-old girl with radiant blue eyes. An automobile accident had left her with a slight limp and a scar on her forehead just at the hairline. Her record had let me know that her academic functioning level was low, but it said nothing about how hard she tried or how deep her desire was to learn. None of the labels I had conferred upon Katy had prepared me for a year of progress for her and countless rewards for me. I was guilty of "personcide," also known in education as "labelism."

The truth is that as teachers we are all guilty of labelism. We refer to youngsters as "my ADD kid," "my three MR's," or "the gifted one." We replace a name with a label and therefore a person with an opinion. It's a "professionally correct" form of name-calling.

Jesus had some strong words about name-calling. He said in Matthew 5 that such could bring you under judgment or direct you to punishment. Jesus specifically mentioned the names "fool" and "Raca," which means moron. I have avoided these words all of my life, but my list of replacement words is long. Jesus' point was not, of course, the use of those specific words. He knew that words flow from our hearts. He would have us use words that place value upon people, not judgment. In Katy's case, the labels were right, but my heart was wrong.

Let's take care, fellow teachers, of the labels we toss around so freely. Sometimes they stick. Sometimes they're wrong. Sometimes, even though they are correct, they come from a heart that wants approval or attention from colleagues. And how many times do we place limits on students by responding to the labels they wear? Let's let Katy be Katy. No label, no problem.

 Career Options

> *"Where did this man get this wisdom and these miraculous powers?" they asked. "Isn't this the carpenter's son?"*
>
> MATTHEW 13:54-55

Sometimes I think I would like to be a carpenter. When a carpenter goes to work in the morning, he looks at a blueprint or hears a foreman say, "Build this wall and that wall and install those windows today." With instructions clear in his mind, he straps on his tool belt and sets to work. Carpenters work hard, and the craftsmanship of a master carpenter is beautiful to see.

I know that a carpenter's work isn't always cut and dried. Building materials don't always cooperate. Angles don't always fit the first time. Perfect days for working outside are rare. Rain, snow, extreme heat, bone-chilling cold, wind, and stifling humidity are more often characteristic of working conditions for carpenters than seventy-two degrees and sunny.

On the other hand, the carpenter's two-by-fours don't ever come from dysfunctional families. Four-by-eight sheets of plywood don't argue with you. Blueprints say what they mean and mean what they say. There has never been a wishy-washy, noncommittal blueprint in a position of leadership. I doubt that there has ever been a carpenter whose heart has been broken by a warped piece of subflooring. I imagine a great sense of satisfaction in starting with an empty lot, and a few months later, walking away from a finished house that someone will call home.

I wonder if Jesus sometimes longed to return to his carpenter shop. I wonder if he ever prayed for God to send him back to a profession that showed visible results every day. I wonder if he wished to go back to planing and smoothing wood instead of shaping the hearts of men.

When people rejected and hated him, did he think of Joseph's hand on his shoulder? Did he hear Joseph saying, "Nice work, Jesus. Go show your mother"?

When his twelve disciples misunderstood him for the hundredth time, did he imagine what it would be like to have twelve apprentice carpenters leaning on his every word? They would have considered him a master and would have followed every instruction to the letter.

Jesus walked out of his carpenter shop and into the teaching profession, never looking back. He answered the call of his Father to reshape the world, not just pieces of wood. Instead of building materials, he was given selfish and stubborn hearts with which to build his kingdom. Jesus taught and taught and never again picked up a hammer, a saw, or a plane. He left a world of meticulous precision and entered one that can blindside, hurt, and disappoint.

If Jesus ever did want to return to his carpenter's tools, he never said so. I would think it fair to say, however, that when for us as teachers the grass looks greener in another profession, Jesus understands. Jesus had done work that was backbreaking, but came here to do work that was sometimes heartbreaking. I would imagine that many days he would have traded his heartache for a good old-fashioned backache.

Sometimes a job that doesn't require me to think, react, make decisions, or care about anyone looks pretty tempting. Some days being an air traffic controller at O'Hare on Christmas Eve sounds less stressful than my job. But before I pack up my desk and give away my bulletin board materials, I have to stop and get very still. Then the whisper comes:

"I have called you to be a teacher. A teacher teaches."

"Thanks for reminding me, Father. I'll be here in the morning."

Brown Bag Covenant

I have eagerly desired to eat this Passover with you.

LUKE 22:15

Ask an elementary student to name his favorite subject in school and you will often hear the same answer: "Recess!" An honest answer to an honest question is refreshing. Recess is, after all, a break from the sit-down, be-quiet, do-your-work atmosphere of the classroom. Ask a teacher to name her favorite time of day, and an honest answer will often be "Lunch!" Thirty minutes of duty-free lunch is, after all, a break from having to make sure that little people sit down, stay quiet, and do their work.

Usually by lunch time, the teachers with whom I work are ready for some conversation with someone over the age of twelve. We spend that precious time discussing the events of the day, venting frustrations, talking about our families, and generally sharing our lives and enjoying each other. Days when deadlines or stacks of paperwork force me to work through lunch, I feel I have really missed something, and I have. I have missed knowing the intimate details of lives that are entwined with mine. I have missed a time to relax and laugh through the quandaries of a day of teaching. I have missed out on friendship's best, a time of covenant relationship.

The connection between food and fellowship is ancient. In Eastern cultures the greeting between friends can be translated, "Have you eaten yet?" The assumption then is if you haven't, we'll eat together.

In New Testament times, the act of eating together actually meant a covenant of friendship. Sharing a meal sealed a commitment to a lifetime of friendship.* No wonder Jesus found himself in so much trouble for eating with tax collectors and sinners. He was promising to be a friend for life to sinners, a perfect picture of who he is for us all.

Jesus even sealed his covenant for eternal life with us with a meal, with wine to gladden our hearts and bread to strengthen us (see Psalm 104:15). He told his disciples that he had "eagerly desired" to eat this Passover with them. Sharing a meal meant friendship to them, but this meal would bring far more than friendship-talk and family-talk. Jesus would fully share his love with them. He would ask them to take him, his body and his blood, fully into themselves. Reclining around the Passover table, they made a commitment to an eternal relationship.

That same table, that same covenant, that same relationship, is offered today. As I participate in the Lord's Supper, I often think of friendships and of meals shared. I think of covenants made for a lifetime. I think of what it means to share a meal with friends. I think of what it means to share a meal with God.

*Charles R. Page II, *Jesus and the Land* (Nashville: Abingdon, 1995), 105.

Remember to Remember

Let us run with perseverance the race marked out for us.
HEBREWS 12:1

I was in line at the grocery store behind an elderly woman I have known all of my life as "Miss Jane." She was a Sunday school teacher in my church as I was growing up and a school teacher by profession. During the course of our conversation I asked her how long she had taught school.

"I taught school for forty-six years," she said. Her smile broadened as she seemed to escape into memories. Returning to reality she said, "Of course, that doesn't include the ten years I substituted after I retired."

Lately, I've been considering my options. Do I want a thirty-year career? What about twenty-five? I can't imagine forty-six years in the classroom, not to mention ten years of substituting. As amazing as a fifty-six-year teaching career is, even more amazing was the soft demeanor that overtook Miss Jane as she spoke. When I said to her that I wasn't sure I could make it quite that long, she said, "Oh, yes, you can. All you have to do is remember how much you love those children. Then you'll go on."

Almost every day it seems that someone says to me, "I don't know that I can do this another ten or fifteen years." The pressures of paperwork, classroom management, children from dysfunctional homes, curriculum upgrades, more paperwork, and on and on, seem to demand more of us than we have to give. Sometimes when we have attended our hundredth in-service, turned in the millionth form in triplicate, or written up the same student for the same behavior for the dozenth time, we forget to remember how much we love those children. We forget to remember how much those children need us. We forget to remember just how important our job is.

I heard a story about a pastor in Guatemala who earned a salary of $80 a month pastoring a small church. He was gifted as a speaker, a leader, and an administrator. The government took note of his talents and offered him a job making ten times the salary he was earning as a pastor. His voice held no hesitation in turning the position down. He thanked them for honoring him with the offer. He said that the salary was great, it was just that the job was too small.

Many people suggest that we teach because we can't do anything else. Perhaps it is just the opposite that is true. We can't do anything else because we teach. Any other job is just too small. Any other job would squeeze us into its mold and leave us with too little influence on the world.

Few of us will finish forty-six years as Miss Jane did, but many of us will finish our thirtieth, or our twenty-fifth, or as many years as life and health will allow. We will finish because we remember to remember. We will finish, not because we cannot, but because we will not do anything else.

Crowded Days

Each day has enough trouble of its own.

MATTHEW 6:34

Mrs. Lane clip-clopped hurriedly to her desk at the front of the room. She was wearing a "Sunday suit" and heels, not the usual attire for an elementary teacher who likes to sit on the floor with her students. She moved quickly from her desk to the chalkboard, to the door of the classroom to talk to another teacher, back to her desk, and then to Andy's desk to help him with his morning work.

Curiosity overtook Samuel.

"Mrs. Lane," he said with his forehead wrinkled, "why are you all dressed up and in such a hurry?"

"I guess I do look a little dressy today," Mrs. Lane responded, smoothing her wool jacket. She held up her daily planner for all to see and explained, "See all of these places that are filled in on my calendar today? Those are all things I have to do. At 10:00 this morning, I have a meeting with all of the other second-grade teachers. At 11:30, the school board is coming to school for lunch and I am the faculty hostess. At 1:00, we have Mr. Marbury, the beekeeper, coming to our classroom. After school there is a faculty meeting. When I leave here, I have to go to the funeral home because my best friend's uncle died. After that I have two meetings at church that are both scheduled at the same time."

"Mrs. Lane," said Samuel, "you have a very crowded day."

Most of us have a preferred way of dealing with the crowdedness that slips into our lives uninvited. Different kinds of crowdedness bring a variety of responses from me. Crowded elevators, for example, are something that I tolerate. The discomfort is short-lived, and the elevator takes me to a desired destination. My response to a crowded restaurant is quite the opposite. If I don't have to be there, why stay? I don't go shopping on Christmas Eve. I don't push through a crowd to look at anybody famous.

But what about that unavoidable crowded day, when the hours are elbow to elbow and I am dizzy, spinning from one thing to another? I usually try to treat those days the same way I deal with a crowded party. A crowded party doesn't seem so crowded if I enjoy it one person at a time. A crowded day doesn't squeeze in around me if I welcome each event one by one. If I am prepared for the day, I can actually enjoy it and meet its conclusion with a sense of accomplishment.

Crowded days will come. If my response is disconnected tolerance, it will show up on my face and in my work, and it will give me an attitude that makes me tired. If I could respond with avoidance (and I'm not sure avoidance is even an option), I would have to stay home and pretend to be sick. Rather, for my crowded days, I will choose to respond to one event at a time, one responsibility at a time.

Shelter for My Soul

You have been a refuge for the poor, a refuge for the needy in his distress, a shelter from the storm and a shade from the heat.

ISAIAH 25:4

Standing on the front porch of a country "Mom and Pop" grocery store, the aroma of Tennessee red clay filled my senses and captured my memory. Suddenly, in my mind, I was transported to a place from my childhood, a place of shelter and shade. Memory took me to my grandparents' stormhouse.

The stormhouse was hardly a house at all. It was a hole dug into the side of a moss-covered hill just behind my grandparents' house. The outside entrance was protected by a tin roof. Wooden steps led down rough, splinter-giving walls to the inner door. Behind it was a place of absolute safety. The tiny room with a red clay floor was impenetrable by anything nature chose to hurl in its direction. No wind, no bolt of lightning, and no flooding rain could intrude upon this underground refuge.

My grandfather had built benches along the walls of the room. The little town where my father grew up was hit by a violent tornado when my dad was a boy. The memory of that storm was unerasable. So when the winds roared and the thunder rumbled, the people came and huddled shoulder to shoulder until nature had had its say. I remember lying with my head in my mother's lap, confident that I was completely safe as the clouds threw a tantrum outside.

Besides being a place of refuge from the storm, the stormhouse was also a storeroom for my grandmother's

131

home-canned fruits and vegetables. A banquet of my favorite foods peeked through hundreds of jars lining shelves above my head. Colorful quarts of pickles, peaches, tomatoes, peas, and green beans all assured me that a feast was always just a hot stove away. In the summer, after a long day of canning in a hot kitchen, I would help my grandfather store away the day's labor. We would drink in the room's fresh coolness, keeping count of each jar we placed on the shelf. In this room, I was safe from both fury and famine. I was certain I was loved, cared for, and protected.

I'm no longer a child. I cannot go to that clay-scented room anymore, but my soul longs for its enveloping assurance. Life rages and deprives. In the midst of fear and want, Jesus has invited me to know him, the one whose words calmed the storm, the one whose power multiplied food for thousands, the one who has given the gift of peace and the promise of living water. He has invited me to live in a place of absolute safety, a stormhouse for my soul.

"Remain in me," he said, "and I will remain in you" (Jn 15:4).

A Word of Grace

Your love has given me great joy and encouragement, because you, brother, have refreshed the hearts of the saints.

PHILEMON 7

Kelly walked into the school building with her head bowed—perhaps against the coldness of the wind, perhaps against the coldness of her heart. In her mind she knew that no one knew what she had done the night before, or rather what had been done to her. But her heart was screaming, "They all know!"

Many times Kelly had decided just to stay home, but there were too many absences and not enough excuses anymore. She couldn't go to the school nurse. There would be too many questions. Kelly wasn't too sure that there was a God anywhere around, but she whispered a prayer just in case.

"Help me to look normal, act normal, and someday please let me feel normal."

Kelly was going to have another tormenting day—that is, until her English teacher, Mrs. Little, spoke to her.

"Good morning, Kelly. I'm so glad you're here. You're going to love our new poetry unit." Kelly felt the corners of her mouth turning upward. Her heart was changed in twenty seconds, because someone spoke a word of grace.

Bobby wrestled with his coat in the hallway. It was too little anyway and too hard to get off. His face was growing redder and redder. Why did Mommy and Daddy have to fight last night? He was so tired. He could never go to sleep when all of the yelling was going on. The fights always started because there wasn't enough money. If it weren't for him, there would be plenty of money. "Stupid coat!"

"Bobby, let me help you with that. There now, I'm looking for a helper this morning, and you're just the one I had in mind. You're the best messenger I know."

Bobby's life was changed, at least for that day, in thirty seconds. His teacher spoke a word of grace.

Mrs. Jones stayed in her car fiddling with some papers in the front seat so it would appear she had a purpose in sitting there. She didn't know if she could smile another courteous smile, speak another warm "Good morning," or stand before another classroom full of students who needed her when she had absolutely nothing left to give. Her mother's long-term illness had sapped every ounce of her strength. It wasn't that she minded getting up with her mother three or four times a night. It was just that she needed a full night's sleep. She needed a walk in the sunshine and a good, long cry.

Summoning her strength and opening the door, she made the long walk up the sidewalk to the yawning front doors of the school. She unexpectedly felt an arm slide around her shoulders. Someone spoke a word of grace.

"You look beat, Lynn. Let's grab a cup of coffee and find a place to talk. I've made a few phone calls, and I think I've found you some inexpensive nighttime help."

A word of grace becomes a ray of hope, a gift of love. We can give these gifts today.

Hand Towels and Toenail Clippers

*Now that I, your Lord and Teacher, have washed your feet, you
also should wash one another's feet. I have set you an example that
you should do as I have done for you.*

JOHN 13:14-15

Jesus was always doing something that had never been
done before, stirring up a variety of reactions. In John 13,
however, Jesus did something that was done every day,
hundreds of times, but it was still shocking. He did what
no one else in the room had even considered doing. He
washed his disciples' feet.

Feet were a most unpleasant body part in Jesus' world.
They were exposed to dirt, mud, and whatever else had
been deposited in the street by people or animals. The tasks
of dealing with feet were left to the lowest-ranked slave or
servant in the house. Jesus chose this lowest position and
most menial task to show his disciples—and us—how to go
about the business of loving each other.

Bill was a retired teacher. He spent his career teaching
history and caring deeply for high school seniors. When he
retired, Bill missed being involved in the students' lives and
making a difference. He needed, and soon found, an outlet
for his caring energy. He began visiting the shut-ins from
his church. He especially enjoyed his time with Miss Mary,
a fellow retired teacher. They would swap stories for hours,
laughing, even crying sometimes.

An unexpected surgery halted Bill's visits for a number of

weeks. He looked forward to visiting Miss Mary again. Bill knocked on her door a first time and then a second time. He heard her familiar voice from way back in the kitchen: "Come on in. It's open." What a shock to see his friend in a wheelchair.

"Miss Mary, what in the world happened?"

"It's my feet, Bill. They hurt so badly I can hardly walk. I drug out this old thing to get me by until I can see a doctor."

"Do you mind if I have a look?" Bill was always a gentleman. Miss Mary nodded in approval, and Bill sank to his knees. He ever so gently removed one house shoe and then the other. What he saw filled his heart with compassion. Miss Mary's arthritic hands had prevented her from cutting her toenails. The nails had grown over the ends of her toes, curved under, and were cutting into the bottoms of her feet.

Bill found a large pan and filled it with warm water. Placing the pan in front of Miss Mary, he invited her to a soothing soak. He reached in his pocket, took out a nail clipper, and set to work relieving Miss Mary's misery. He clipped, he rinsed, and he massaged. When he finished, he dried each foot with a towel, took Miss Mary by the hand, and helped her out of the wheelchair.

Bill had done what no one else had bothered to do. He had shown her the full extent of his love. Miss Mary, for the first time in weeks, walked to the stove and made a pot of tea to share with her friend.

When I think of serving others, I often pray, "Lord, make me a toenail clipper."

Indivisible Under God

I have given them the glory that you gave me, that they may be one as we are one.

JOHN 17:22

The last Friday before spring break may just be the longest day of the school year. Our calendar has a long "dry spell" of five-day weeks between Christmas and Easter. It's hard to tell who needs the break more—the students or the teachers. A couple of years ago, I was especially anxious for the Friday dismissal bell, knowing that very special guests would arrive at my house that afternoon.

The Kylanders, our best friends, had moved to Ohio three years ago. Since then, our time together has been limited to phone calls and a yearly visit. Spring break with them brought sun-warmed days and porch-sitting nights. Our house was filled with friendship, good food, laughter, and five stair-step boys.

Mandy and I planted my flower beds. She picked out and pointed where; I unpotted and planted. The two dads spent "guy time" together. The *Lion King* reigned on the television, and my two boys savored the opportunity to be "big brothers" to her three children.

Friendship lasts a lifetime, but spring break lasts only a week.

Saying good-bye to good friends is always difficult. Sunday came, and the five hundred miles that usually separate us made their demand. The Kylander van pulled out of our driveway, headed north, and we returned to a four-person household. For a while, it seemed that the house itself yearned to be filled again.

Later that day, I was returning from a replenishing trip to the grocery store. My mind was on the week ahead and the return to what we call normal. The words of a song on the radio met my distracted brain. They called me back to the commitment in friendship, the importance of praying for one another, and the difference Jesus makes.

Unexpectedly, warm wetness rolled down my face. I never cry when the Kylanders leave. Distance and time barriers are just a part of our relationship. Tears came anyway, dripping from my chin, blurring my vision. My tears came because of the realization of two realities.

One is the reality of the world in which we live: stoplights and speed limits, timed tests, parking spaces, and boundary lines. In this world, we are limited by time and space. The second reality is that we have been given gifts that know no bounds of distance or time, from a God who transcends them both.

We have been given the gift of love and the privilege of prayer. As surely as I am bound to obey the visible boundaries of the road I am traveling, I am bound invisibly, profoundly, to the five people who at that moment were moving farther and farther away from me. The Kylanders' van sped them on to Ohio, and mine rolled me home to normalcy, but the detachment of miles paled in comparison to the connection of love and prayer.

Surprise Packages

For you created my inmost being; you knit me together in my mother's womb. I praise you because I am fearfully and wonderfully made.

PSALM 139:13-14

My friend, Dr. Kathy Koch, founder of the ministry *Celebrate Kids, Inc.*, often says it is important to take a good look at the things that got us in trouble as children. They might just be the same things that earn us a living as adults. Though Kathy is known as "Dr. Kathy" now, she was called "Chatty Kathy" as a little girl. This one who once caused so much disruption in the classroom now makes her living as a public speaker.

The same principle is true for me. My eighth-grade English teacher wrote a comment on one of my compositions that I will never forget. At the top of the page, in red ink, were these words: "You have a flair for writing, but you need to use more words."

Mrs. McKamey's words of affirmation were encouraging to me, but I have always found it frustrating to stretch my thoughts into more words than I believe are necessary. Little did Mrs. McKamey or I know that, one day, my ability to be brief and concise would land me a contract to write a devotional book.

It's fun to imagine my students turning the very characteristics that drive me up a wall into gainful employment. I think of Elizabeth, the busy one who never lands in one place for long. As a waitress, she would be a restaurant owner's dream. At her assigned tables, customers would never be waiting or wondering where their waitress was. She would be busy and visible.

Patrick, who raises his hand every two minutes, just to be sure he is doing his work correctly, is just the kind of person I want piloting when I fly. Give me a pilot like Patrick who checks and triple checks.

It would be Anna, my little Miss Neatnick, whom I would choose as my surgeon. She keeps every paper straight, every pencil sharpened, every hair in place. Nary a germ would dare to enter her operating room.

And then there's Heath. Nothing, absolutely nothing, seems to bother him—not even Elizabeth's hyperactivity, Patrick's persnickityness, or Anna's continuous rearranging. Neither is he upset by sudden changes in schedule, visitors in our room, or mood swings in his teachers and friends. I hope Heath becomes a teacher and teaches in the classroom right next door.

Sometimes those things that we think are curses just might be gifts. Maybe, just maybe, we can turn a negative into a positive. A weakness channeled in the right direction just might become a strength. What would happen if we looked at it that way?

A Warm Reminder

You have given me the heritage of those who fear your name.

PSALM 61:5

Just after Christmas 1992, my parents and my aunt and uncle were faced with the task of cleaning out my grandparents' home. They were both gone now. Grandmother had died that fall, and my grandfather, six years earlier. A cousin had purchased the house, and we now needed to make way for the "homeplace" to become a new home.

One cold afternoon, my mom and I were clearing away small items from the house. Occasionally one of us would say, "Look at this," and discovery would take us to memory. We found my grandfather's glasses that he had worn when I was just a child. We discovered an unopened package of chewing tobacco in the back of the dresser drawer. It must have been the last one my grandfather bought before he decided to give it up. My grandmother's Sunday school book, with answers written in, lay on the table beside her chair.

My mother's comment, "What in the world?" called me into the bedroom where she was working. She had retrieved a paper sack from the bottom of an antique chifforobe. Reaching into the sack, she took out an old dinner plate, the kind that came as a bonus in a box of laundry detergent in the sixties. The plate was badly chipped in several places.

Mom held the plate carefully and gazed long at each side. Her eyes were filled with tears when she handed it to me. On the serving side of the plate in my grandfather's handwriting were these words: "Jeffrey [my son] broke his first plate, April 1985, Big Granddaddy's house." And on the back, "By the time you get this plate, I hope you are big enough to hold your plate. Ha, Ha, E.R. Abbott."

We had not enjoyed my grandfather's humor in over six years, and its unexpected appearance brought a mixture of laughter and tears. For a treasured moment, Granddaddy Abbott was present with us. We knew him well, and we knew that his well-planned message meant far more than the words on the plate. It was as if he were saying to us, "Remember me. Remember how I loved life. Remember how I loved you. I'll see you soon." The one who had gone warmed our day by that which remained.

Not so different is the message of our heavenly Father. Through his Word, through his Son, and through a holy meal he says to us, "Remember me. Remember that I created all life. Remember how I love you. I'll see you soon." May we dwell today in the warmth of his reminder.

The Memory Business

I thank my God every time I remember you.

PHILIPPIANS 1:3

I have a friend who says he is in the memory business. He is a photographer. During the course of my lifetime, whenever there has been an event to be remembered, Mitch has been there, ready to capture it on film. He took my high school graduation pictures, my wedding pictures, my sorority formal pictures, and even now continues to do whatever photography work I need. Mitch is very good at what he does, and he takes his business seriously. After all, the slice of life trapped in his camera will be transferred to paper and shared for generations. I'm glad he doesn't take it lightly.

We as teachers are in the memory business, too, and maybe even more profoundly so. The memories we help to shape are entrapped in the minds and souls of the youngsters we teach. When I put my brain on rewind and search for memories of my school days, I am able to pinpoint some very specific events. I remember watching Alan Shepard's first flight into space on black-and-white television at school. I remember my second-grade teacher hobbling around the classroom on crutches, thanks to a broken leg. I remember being slapped in the face by one teacher and embraced by another. I remember my Spanish teacher jumping around the room as she acted out portions of *El Cid*. I remember a junior high math teacher throwing an eraser at a sleeping young man in the back of the room. I remember my teacher's tears when we learned of the assassination of John Kennedy. I remember a teacher's quick response to a broken arm on the playground.

My gray matter is filled with memories installed by teachers. Some are funny, and some are serious. Some bring a smile to my face; some leave me cold. Overshadowing specific memories of each grade and subject, however, is an overall impression of each teacher. I remember Miss Kelly's tenderness, Miss Marberry's calmness, Mrs. Wilson's mood swings, and Mr. Arrington's encouragement. I remember an algebra teacher's patience and a history teacher's complacency.

I have heard it said that students will remember 10 percent of what you say, 20 percent of what you do, and 100 percent of who you are. It is interesting to consider what my students' 10- and 20-percent memories might be. What will they remember of what I have said? What have I done that they will never forget? But it is downright convicting to think about what they will remember of who I am.

We are in the memory business as surely as my photographer friend. The difference? He captures them. We create them.

Something in Common

Teach [these words] to your children, talking about them when you sit at home and when you walk along the road, when you lie down and when you get up.

DEUTERONOMY 11:19

Touring a brand new school in another part of our state, I was in awe of such a fabulous facility. The design, the setup, and the technology were beyond anything I had ever seen.

We passed by a kindergarten classroom where the teacher was seated in a rocking chair, reading a story to twenty expectant little faces. The spacious room allowed for a reading center at the back with carpet and beanbag chairs.

Down another hall, the walls of a third-grade classroom were lined with computers, all winking their screen savers as the teacher pointed to a map on a big-screen TV in the front of the room. All eyes were on the monster screen as the teacher explained the location of Puget Sound.

Fifth-grade students were working in cooperative groups as the teacher and an assistant circulated around another room. The students' desks were specially designed to facilitate group work. There was plenty of room for the teachers to move around in the classroom.

If this sounds like a little bit of heaven, perhaps it was. Yet for all of the technology and design, those classrooms all had one thing in common with my grandmother's one-room schoolhouse ... a teacher. The single most important factor in any classroom is you, the teacher.

Imagine another school. The building is fifty years old, with green-tile floors and plaster walls. The lighting has been updated and new acoustic ceilings installed, but nothing disguises the old plumbing and the unreliable heating system.

As you pass by a kindergarten classroom, the teacher is seated in her desk chair with the students surrounding her. She is reading a story to twenty expectant little ones seated on carpet samples.

The third-grade class is in the middle of a social studies lesson. The teacher pulls down a map that has been hanging there for twenty-five years to show her class the location of Puget Sound. She visited there last year, and her description of the ferry ride and the refreshing breeze has her students smelling salty air and feeling the breeze.

In the fifth grade, all of the desks have been pushed against the wall so the class can sit on the floor to work in cooperative groups. The teacher and the assistant are both seated on the floor, scooting from group to group, laughing and scooting, making children smile.

The greatest teacher of all time didn't have much of a classroom. He walked around the countryside followed by a group of his students. He taught from the steps of the temple. He taught on a mountainside, from a boat, and in the courtyard of someone's home. Wherever Jesus went, he was teaching and looking for teachable moments with his students. No classroom, no materials, no—*absolutely no*—technology.

If you teach in one of those top-notch, high-tech schools, bless you!! If you teach in a run-down facility that needs new everything, bless you, too!! You share the profession of the Master Teacher.... Teach on!!

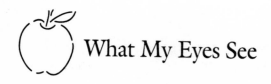 # What My Eyes See

I will lift up my eyes to the hills—where does my help come from?

"WHAT MY EYES SEE"

She called them flowers;
I called them weeds
and said, "I'll have to mow them down,
    Before they scatter
    Too many seeds
    All over the ground."

She looked at me
And cried, "Let them be
    If you please.
    They may just be weeds to you,
    But that's not what my eyes see."

The world calls them worthless.
He says, "They're whole.
    Don't mow them down
    And shatter
    Too many souls
    And leave them lying on the ground."

He looked at me
And cried, "Let them be
    If you please.
    They may seem worthless
    To all the world
    But that's not what my eyes see."

I call Him King
They say, "He deceives."
> And they'll have to mow him down
> Before he scatters
> Too many seeds
> All around.

He looked at me.
I cried, "Let him be
> If you please.
> He may not be
> A King to you,
> But that's not what my eyes see."

Connie Taylor, 1994

Every spring my friend Jan and I make a trip to a local greenhouse and nursery. She buys flowers. I buy herbs. She leaves the nursery with arm-loads of color. I leave with a few spindly green sprigs. She laughs and says that I am paying money for weeds. I know better.

The beauty of the flowers in front of her house is breathtaking. The beauty of my herbs is known only in steeping tea or simmering sauce. Sometimes a weed is not a weed at all. It simply needs to be nurtured and given a chance to share its beauty.

# Joy Connection

I have told you this so that my joy may be in you and that your joy may be complete.

JOHN 15:11

Our Monday afternoon Bible study lesson was on the topic of joy. The group, made up mostly of teachers, talked about joy as a state of mind and about joy as something we experience.

Afterward, one of my friends hung around so that she could walk out with me. She is in a difficult teaching situation, with a high-profile, politically active administration. Furthermore, her personal life has not exactly been one in which she could skip along throwing flower petals behind her.

"I guess I have really missed the boat with this joy thing," she said.

"Why?"

"Well, I understand about joy as a state of mind, tied closely with hope and peace," she answered. "But the experience part seems a million miles away." Then she asked me a penetrating question. "Can you remember the last time you experienced joy?"

What if I asked you the same question. When was the last time you experienced joy?

Many of us think of joy as an experience reserved for children. If you are an elementary teacher, you might be able to get a glimpse of experiential joy today. Watch the little children on the swings or merry-go-round. You will see heads-thrown-back abandonment and embraced-by-the-sun, refreshed-by-the-wind joy.

Maybe you don't have to go to a playground. Maybe your memory can take you there.

For many little children, experiential joy comes daily. As adults, we often give joy entrance into our lives only in major events: the birth of a child, our marriage, winning the championship game. We seem to think that joy is reserved for the high points. Many of us have forgotten to seek joy daily.

Jesus desires joy for all of his Father's children. Joy comes to us through abiding in the love of Christ, living moment by moment in affectionate connection to him. Jesus said, "As the Father has loved me, so have I loved you. Now remain in my love" (Jn 15:9). Later in that same chapter, he explained his reason for telling us to remain in his love. He told us to remain in his love so that our "joy may be complete." Complete joy is inseparably connected to living in the love of Christ.

Life's bumps and bruises take away my desire to throw my head back in laughter, to allow myself the privilege of mindless abandonment, but I can still steal away to an affectionate place of joy. That place for me is an inseparable connection to the love of Christ.

Have I experienced joy lately? Absolutely yes! His joy abiding in me and my abiding in his love.

When was the last time you experienced joy?

Moderation in Moderation

I know your deeds, that you are neither cold nor hot. I wish you were either one or the other! So, because you are lukewarm—neither hot nor cold—I am about to spit you out of my mouth.

REVELATION 3:15-16

I have a friend whose motto in life is "Everything in moderation." It sounds biblical and profound when applied to some of life's basics. If I eat in moderation, I will never have a weight problem or any of the health issues that arise from excess weight. If I drink in moderation, I will not become dependent on alcohol or commit some awful offense while under its influence. If I exercise in moderation, though I will never be a winner in competition, I will not risk injury or be overly fatigued.

I would love to do a moderate amount of housework and spend a moderate amount of time gardening and doing yard work. I wish that Saturdays were moderately free of grocery shopping and errand running. I can be satisfied with a moderately nice car which I drive at a moderate speed. I long for a moderate amount of laundry and dishes to do. But, *everything* in moderation?

I do not wish to be moderately fed, moderately loved, or moderately rested. I don't want to be seated on an airplane next to someone who practices moderation in bathing and teeth brushing. I do not want to attend a church whose minister does a moderate amount of preparation on his sermons or where moderation in worship is encouraged. I do not enjoy food that has been moderately flavored by a moderately good cook. I do not want a moderate marriage with moderate children, nor do I want friendships with a moderate investment. I do not want to be a moderately good teacher whose students do moderately well. And when my time on earth is done, I do not want to hear my Lord say, "Moderately well done, thou moderately good and moderately faithful servant."

Perhaps I should suggest to my friend that moderation is a good measuring stick for anything in life that can potentially do us harm, or that requires no passion. I can measure the amount of food I eat with moderation, but give me zesty flavor. I may not work out every day, but when I am out there, let me sweat and strain as though my life depended on it.

My work requires balance of time and energy, but may I never be only moderately interested in teaching or in learning. Relationships may need to be held to a moderate number, but deliver me from dispassionate connection in marriage, family, and friendships. May I never choose moderation in my spiritual life. May I pray with passion, love others deeply, sing from my heart, and earnestly desire to know my God. Our God is a God of passion. May I passionately serve.

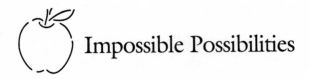 Impossible Possibilities

The disciples ... asked, "Who then can be saved?" Jesus looked at them and said, "With man this is impossible, but with God all things are possible."

MATTHEW 19:25-26

"Linda, I need to see you in my office when you get a chance." The tone of our guidance counselor's voice convinced me not to wait too long to see what she wanted. Half an hour or so later, I found time to walk around to her office. I found the door open and Kathy working at her desk.

"It's about Billy," she said as I closed the door behind me. "I just happened to be in a store last night as he was being arrested. One deputy sheriff was handcuffing him while another was counting out cash they had found on Billy. I don't know all of the details, but someone caught him red-handed, stealing money from the cash register. I just wanted you to hear it from me and not read it on the front page of the paper in the morning."

My heart sank. Billy had been a student of mine for three years. He had driven every teacher he had ever had straight up a wall, and he didn't exactly leave my feet on the floor either. But he had stolen my heart and he knew it. I just wish he had been content with heart thievery.

Every year, Billy was caught stealing something at school, and each year the crime was a little more serious. He had gone from taking candy from the Halloween carnival to stealing money from the PTO. He was always punished and made to pay back what he had stolen. I remember telling him when he was in the fifth grade to consider another hobby; even putting morality aside, he just wasn't good enough at stealing to make it profitable. Fifth grade had long since passed and my advice had gone unheeded.

When I think about Billy and his future, part of me wants to just say, "Forget it. You gave him your best. You can't change a leopard's spots, teach an old dog new tricks, or fool Mother Nature."

But then I consider what Jesus had to say when the rich young ruler turned him down flat. Jesus suggested to this young man also that he consider another hobby—poverty. Jesus' suggestion went unheeded as well, and the young man turned away. Scripture tells us that the young man was sad about it, but not sad enough. I can just imagine the contemplative look in Jesus' eyes as he watched him walk away.

"It is easier for a camel to go through the eye of a needle than for a rich man to enter the kingdom of God," he said to his disciples. The disciples found Jesus' words troubling.

"Who then can be saved?" they asked.

Perhaps Jesus' eyes were still following the one who rejected him. Maybe he knew something wonderful that the disciples did not know. Maybe, even then, he knew something about Billy.

"With man this is impossible," he said, "but with God all things are possible."

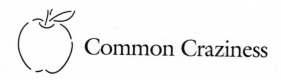 # Common Craziness

Who has measured the waters in the hollow of his hand, or with the breadth of his hand marked off the heavens?

ISAIAH 40:12

The message on my answering machine was brief, but it brought a smile to my face. "Linda, I have just read Kathy's newsletter. It sounded so much like you! Call me and let's talk about it."

The voice on my answering machine was referring to a bimonthly newsletter from our mutual friend, Kathy Bearce. Kathy is a counselor for missionaries with World Team Missions. Kathy's letter spoke of life as a journey, of living and loving, of pain endured and joys granted.

Of course it sounded like me. Kathy and I—and you— share the same final destination in this journey we call life. It is this common destination, our eternal perspective, our "way of thinking," our "worldview," that makes us the same. Though we stumble into different potholes, carry different burdens, and wander off on different rabbit trails, we all are granted the same Spirit who directs us as we travel. The things that make us the same make us radically different from the rest of the world.

The truth is that many we meet in the course of our journey find us to be a little crazy, a little out of our minds. Paul speaks of this in 2 Corinthians 5:13: "If we are out of our mind, it is for the sake of God."

A couple of summers ago, our Bible study group decided

to look into this "craziness," to examine our way of thinking. We found that a line can be clearly drawn between our worldview and that of our unbelieving friends. We called it "Kingdom Thinking" versus "World Thinking." The more we learned, the bolder the line became. More and more, we came to realize that we were forever changed by the greatness of God and the love of Christ. How could we not be the same? How could we not be different? That summer I learned to enjoy my difference and the "insanity" of my journey.

In my journal I wrote, "Walking on a beach, playing tag with the waves, I am overwhelmed with thoughts of the vastness of the ocean. I capture salt water in my cupped hand and wonder just where this water has been and what secrets it could tell. Have these waves kissed the bow of a massive ship or been spouted skyward by a humpback whale? Will these waters fly to the heavens and join a cloud? Will these moist molecules water a garden in England or an oasis in the desert? How can I see such wonder and not think of the God who created it all? In the hollow of his hand he can hold all of the oceans of the earth. If I am crazy, let me be so for the sake of an awesome and powerful God."

Maybe my journal sounds a lot like yours. Maybe you have had the same thoughts, the same questions. We do have the same destination, you know, and we share the same "craziness."

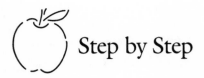 Step by Step

Forgetting what is behind and straining toward what is ahead, I press on toward the goal to win the prize for which God has called me heavenward in Christ Jesus.

PHILIPPIANS 3:13-14

When I first started running, twenty years ago, I could see progress every day. My first "run" started from my front porch and ended at the corner stop sign, a distance of about fifty yards. It was a heart-pounding, breathtaking experience. The next day, I ran to the stop sign and around the corner a few yards. After that, I ran a little farther each day until I was running a one-mile loop. I felt a sense of accomplishment that had been missing from my life for some time. By just taking a few steps down the street, that sense of accomplishment returned. Progress is so sweet.

Once running had become a part of my life and my mileage was up to twenty miles or so in a week, progress didn't come as quickly or as easily. I was still able to set my sights on a distance goal and accomplish it, but goals took longer to reach and I had to train harder. My sense of accomplishment on some days came from just finishing the course. A cool glass of water and relaxing fatigue were a delightful reward.

I ran right through my first pregnancy. I must have looked like a front-end loader moving down the street, but I had great legs. The birth of my first son brought an end to my running schedule as I then knew it, and it hasn't been the same since. A second child brought a layoff of several years, and, oh, what a difference those years made. When I started running again, progress no longer came quickly. I was no longer in my twenties, and my body knew it. None of my body parts functioned as well as they once had. Three miles forward, two miles back. Progress began to mean something entirely different to me.

Today, progress is just getting out there and putting one foot in front of the other. Most days, I measure progress in mailboxes. My distance goal is to make it to the next mailbox. When I get there, then I can decide about making it to the one after that. Progress is small, one mailbox at a time, but still sweet.

The teaching profession is a bit like training for running. Many of us began our teaching careers with hopes of changing the world, of seeing progress every day. Some days it happens. Some days they all "get it." Many days, however, we wonder what made us think today would make a difference. Maybe what you did today didn't make the evening news, but it still counted for progress. Maybe they won't be handing you the Teacher of the Year award, but when you lock your door in June, you will have changed the world. Not in sweeping strides of marathon proportions, but in the best way it can be changed, one youngster at a time. The only way to change a youngster is one day at a time. Progress, however slow, is indeed so sweet.

A Little Peace and Noise, Please

Jesus often withdrew to lonely places.

LUKE 5:16

Ask most people to name their favorite place and the answer will be something like Hawaii, the beach, the mountains, a cabin in the woods, Paris, or even Mom's front porch. The names of a few of my favorite places sound really sophisticated and artsy, but I can't go to them very often. If you were to look for me in one of my unsophisticated, extremely unartsy, favorite places, you would find me sitting under a salon hairdryer or on my riding lawnmower.

Before you picture me as a Steel Magnolia at the local beauty parlor, however, let me say that I only gain possession of the seat under the dryer when Becky does a certain treatment to my hair every ten weeks or so. As for the lawnmower, it is unfortunate that one of my favorite places is also a tool for teaching my sons the value of work. Whenever I can, however, I sweetly volunteer to mow the lawn so my sons can be free to do something they want to do.

The common thread between the hairdryer and the lawnmower is constant, steady, loud noise. Constant, steady, loud noise means no distractions. I can't hear the telephone, the neighbor's dog, the radio, or the hair clippers. You have to bang on the hairdryer to get my attention or jump up and down and wave your arms when I am on the lawnmower.

Jesus used to go to a "lonely place" to be away from distractions. No quiet mountainside is waiting in my backyard. Neither is there a garden with only the sound of singing birds and rustling leaves. I live in a four-bedroom, two-story nest of disruption. There isn't a lonely place in it. Something or somebody always needs ironing, feeding, cleaning, or finding, and I seem to be the only one who can do it right. At school, disruptions are a way of life. I can't seem to finish what I need to do for taking care of what I have to do. A battle rages between urgency and importance, and neither seems to win. The intercom disrupts my teaching and my train of thought about a hundred times a day with messages that I needed to know yesterday.

Is it any wonder that I enjoy hairdryer-lawnmower solitude? My world seems to call me to a "noisy" place just as often as to a lonely place. Don't misunderstand. I will head for the mountains and the solitude of a roaring stream whenever I can. I will answer the call of the ocean and the beach whenever my schedule allows. More often than that, however, I will escape to one of my places of noisy detachment. Right now, I think my lawn needs mowing.

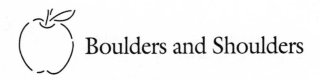

Boulders and Shoulders

Carry each other's burdens, and in this way you will fulfill the law of Christ.

GALATIANS 6:2

Traveling through the mountains of East Tennessee, there is a sign beside the highway that I find a bit disturbing. WATCH FOR FALLING ROCK. I have been to the Smoky Mountains many times and have seen neither boulder nor pebble descend upon some unsuspecting vehicle, but the sign is still troubling. Occasionally, I see a monster stone resting at the highway's edge and I know it did not grow there, nor was it placed there by some Boulder Preservation Society. It stands in validation of the warning, and it keeps me cowering and looking upward. I know that it fell without warning. I know that it will not be moved easily.

Such was my visual image as I began to study the sixth chapter of Galatians. Paul tells us in verse two that believers fulfill the law of Christ by carrying each other's burdens. The word for burdens there actually means "boulder." "Carry each other's boulders," says Paul. When I read it that way, I picture those gigantic, immovable stones along the side of the mountain highway. "Carry that?" I think. Then I remember, "Oh, yeah, I don't have to carry it alone."

Over the past couple of years, my circle of friends has had to cope with some pretty huge boulders. The death of a husband, the loss of a job, a father with a brain tumor, a mother with breast cancer, the senseless murder of a daughter, unexpected relocation, broken marriages, empty nests, broken finances, and empty hearts are a few of the falling rocks that have come into our lives. As each boulder was encountered, friends circled around to support the one whose path seemed impassable, when going on seemed impossible. Each load has been lifted by a lever of love and placed on as many shoulders as it took to move it along. Some of those shoulders are strong and wide, while others can only help a pebble's worth. Boulder-carrying takes each of us doing whatever we can.

Many have walked heavily and boulders have fallen, but no one has been crushed. Whenever one of us has started to falter and slip under the weight of our load, others have been close by, shoulder to shoulder, to encourage and share the carrying. Often one of us has thought that we could not bear to go another step, but tomorrow has always come, and we have been comforted that we have not had to face it alone. The law of Christ, to love one another, has been fulfilled.

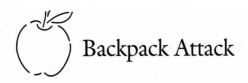 # Backpack Attack

Each one should carry his own load.

I don't carry a purse very often. To my way of thinking, if something doesn't fit in my pocket, I probably don't need it. I do, when necessary, carry a backpack. A backpack is large enough to hold notebooks, pens, books, a billfold, and even my laptop computer. My backpack also keeps me hands-free and mobile. Rummage through my backpack and you will have a pretty good idea of my plans for the day, as well as the general direction of my life. I try to keep my backpack purged of unnecessary items and loaded only with things I will need. When it is overloaded, I cannot carry it very far or very long. Something has to go.

We've already said that Galatians 6:2 tells us to carry one another's burdens—meaning to carry one another's "boulders." But Galatians 6:5 says that we should carry our own loads. That sounds contradictory. How can I carry my own load while I am helping with everyone else's boulders? The word for "load" in Galatians 6:5 literally means "knapsack." Each of us is to carry our own knapsack. As opposed to the heavy and unexpected "boulders" that fall onto our path, our knapsacks are filled with the "rocks" of responsibility that we pick and choose for ourselves. The responsibility for the contents of my knapsack rests directly upon me. If it is bulging, something has to go.

Our Monday afternoon Bible study group has learned to

hold each other accountable with an occasional knapsack check. "Ginger, how many rocks are you carrying in your knapsack these days?" "Your knapsack is bulging, Gerry Ann. Maybe it's time for an inventory."

I have just come through a period when my knapsack was overloaded. The paperwork responsibilities are overwhelming for a special education teacher at the end of the school year. Spring also means baseball at our house. Each son is on a different team with different practices and games. My oldest son plays on a junior PGA golf tour, which requires practice and transportation. My softball coach called to let me know when practice would begin for our women's team. Our house is on the market. I teach two Bible studies, and I have a deadline from my publisher. Add the items that never escape from my knapsack like cooking, cleaning, and laundry, and I have a knee-buckling load.

If I am called to carry my own knapsack, I had better make sure it is carry-able. Some of our rocks have to stay. We can chip away at others by sharing responsibilities. Some can be tossed. The ending of the school year lightened my load considerably. I took a break from teaching Bible study. My husband and sons have arranged transportation to their games and practices. My younger son is helping me with the housework. I painfully decided not to play softball this season, and I am keeping office hours for my writing. I am walking taller with my knapsack these days.

What's in your knapsack?

 Storm Warnings

Out of the brightness of his presence clouds advanced, with hail-stones and bolts of lightning.

PSALM 18:12

I've always had great respect for the wrath of a summer thunderstorm. To be honest, storms were my greatest childhood fear. My grandmother often told me of the time that she had taken shelter in a drainage ditch from a powerful and destructive tornado. Her description of the sound of houses being torn apart and of debris flying through the air left me anticipating the potential power of every approaching storm. She taught me to identify the wispy, white tops of distant wind-storm clouds and the yellow tint of clouds bringing hail. She bequeathed to me a watchful eye when purple clouds roll like tumbleweeds.

Today darkness preceded by those familiar white smoke signals captured the western sky. My stomach knotted as deep rumblings gave way to tree-bending wind. I watched out my bedroom window as the top of my neighbor's newly planted maple tree swept the ground. I listened for warnings on the TV and, with candles in hand, anticipated a loss of power. All of the signs were there. I prepared myself in every way possible for what was about to happen. But for whatever reason, the fury of the front moved eastward as quickly as it came. It left no damage in its wake, no debris, no harm. The storm left behind only a warm gentle rain—the kind in which you can walk and to which you can turn your face.

Sometimes I am a storm, raging and leaving a path of destruction. As a teacher, however, the debris I leave behind cannot be cleared by a bulldozer. It cannot be repaired with wood and nails. My destructive power can tear down imagination, whisk away self-esteem, and annihilate trust. With an off-hand comment or a sigh of frustration I can bring a student's progress to a screeching halt. I can brush a student away like a puff of wind and cause him to never come back to me.

I cannot depend on the National Weather Service for a thunderstorm warning or a tornado watch in my spirit. I have to listen for my rumblings and heed my own darkness. When the winds of frustration begin to blow or a cloud of too much responsibility is on the rise, I had better heed the warning.

It is only in knowing the potential of a coming storm that I am available for transformation, and it is the grace of God alone that can change me into a soothing, healing rain—the kind to which a child can turn his face.

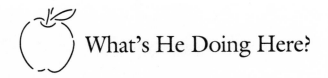 # What's He Doing Here?

I have come that they may have life, and have it to the full.

JOHN 10:10

A couple of summers ago, I flew to Seattle to take a week-long class on the subject of learning styles. One little sideline dynamic was that the class was taught by three women, each of whom measured six feet tall. It hadn't been planned that way; it just happened.

After class the first day, I went to dinner with these three lofty presences. I'm sure we were quite a sight—three oaks and a stump. As we were waiting to be seated in a restaurant, one of the teachers saw someone that she had not seen in awhile. "So, what are you doing here?" her friend asked.

"Oh, we're here with the National Convention for the Tall," she answered, glancing down at the top of my head.

"Really?" said the friend, her eyes assessing my five-feet-four-inch frame. "So what's she doing here?"

"What's she doing here?" A question for someone who is out of place, out of their element, or in the right place at the wrong time. During Jesus' life, I think it is a question that must have been asked many times.

Imagine what the shepherds must have thought, out for a normal evening of protecting their sheep. A sudden angelic visit woke them up for sure. They were told to look for a Savior in, of all places, a manger. They went and found everything just as the angel had said. There he was—

Christ the Lord, a baby lying in a manger. Out of place? Out of his element? What's he doing here?

I would think that Mary and Joseph's introduction to parenting must have been a less than realistic preparation for future children. But there was that one time when Mary found herself scolding Jesus. They were headed home from Jerusalem with a huge crowd of family and friends. They walked all day before discovering that Jesus was missing. Back in Jerusalem they looked for Jesus for two more days. They found him in, of all places, the temple. In the right place at the wrong time? Mary's question to Jesus was her version of "What are you doing here?"

After the magnificent event of Jesus' baptism, he disappeared for a while. He wandered off into the wilderness for fasting, praying, preparing, and communing, but why was he doing it there? Three years later, after teaching, healing, and repeatedly displaying his divinity, he was seen in a most unlikely place. What was a King doing on a cross?

What was Jesus doing anywhere—in a manger, in the temple, in the wilderness, or nailed to a cross? He was out of his holy element, but he was in the right place at the right time, doing what he was called to do, loving us.

Jesus—the baby, the child, the man, the Redeemer—was always where he was supposed to be. Where is he now? What's he doing there? He is seated at the right hand of the Father, still loving us.

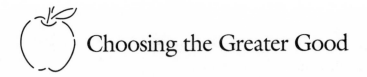

Choosing the Greater Good

If your brother sins, rebuke him, and if he repents, forgive him.

LUKE 17:3

I saw him do it. I sat right there at my desk and watched him cheat on an English test. Jay, a capable student, had chosen an evening at a basketball game over an evening of studying. The temptation to look at the test paper just to his left was too great to resist. After his third look, his eyes met mine. He knew that I knew. I knew that he knew that I knew. The next move was mine, and I had to weigh my options carefully.

I could ignore the whole thing. I could pretend that I didn't see him look at Cynthia's paper and hope that he never did it again. On the other hand, I could make a loud and clear example of Jay. I could snatch up his paper from his desk, pronounce that there would be no cheating in my class, and put a big red zero on his paper for all to see. Though he would be getting what he deserved, he would know that I considered him to be a cheater, his friends would know that he cheated, and he would perceive himself to be a cheater—and not a very good one. My relationship with Jay from that point on would be shame-based on his part, authority-based on mine. My options were denial, punishment, or mercy. I chose mercy.

As the students filed out of my class I asked Jay to stay for a minute. Jay watched as I graded his paper.

"Eighty-five. Not bad," I said. "Jay, I'm going to ask you a question one time, and my next move hinges completely on how you respond. Who deserves this eighty-five, you or Cynthia?"

"I, uh; she, uh ..." Deep breath. "I don't deserve it. I looked at Cynthia's answers." His chin dropped to his chest, his glance to his feet.

"Thank you for being honest with me. You know that the consequence for cheating in our school is a zero on the test and two days of in-school suspension."

"Yes, ma'am."

"Jay, I am choosing to believe that you have never cheated in my class before. I am choosing to believe this is something that you did today, and that it is not a part of your character. I am choosing to believe that you will never cheat in my class again.

"What grade do you think you would have received on this test if you had not looked at Cynthia's answers?" I asked, looking him straight in the eyes.

"About a sixty-five."

"So be it," I declared. "You will have a sixty-five on this test, and the matter is closed. I expect that you will not say a word to anyone about this conversation. You are not a cheater, Jay. You simply chose to try cheating today. It didn't work, and I expect you to remember that. You are not a liar. You proved that by telling me the truth. I deeply value honesty, and I value you as a young man of integrity. When you leave here today, continue to be exactly that."

He did.

I share this story because we are constantly talking to our students about choices. We teach them that each choice directs the rest of their lives, but sometimes it is our response to their choices that brings about direction. Fellow teacher, weigh your responses well. You will be directing a future.

 # Sunday Hungry

Blessed are those who hunger and thirst for righteousness, for they will be filled.

MATTHEW 5:6

When I was growing up, we would visit my grandparents about every two weeks or so, usually on Sunday for lunch. The aroma of my grandmother's culinary craft would escape from the kitchen window and capture me as soon as I stepped out of the car. I knew that my favorite meal was waiting for me on the kitchen table. I have the same memory over and over of my grandmother coming out of the kitchen, wiping her hands on her apron, and throwing her arms around me.

"I was a-gettin' awful hungry to see you," she would say. Even as a child I understood exactly what she meant. She wanted to see me as much as I was ready to dive into some of her fried chicken and mashed potatoes. The hunger was intense, but satisfaction was fabulous!

I haven't experienced that Sunday hunger in a long time. In fact, hunger itself is harder and harder to come by. We live in a culture that greatly discourages hunger. Commercial after commercial on television tempts us with some little delight that will keep away the stomach snarls between meals. Weight-loss products promise not just to help us drop unwanted pounds but to spare us the feeling of hunger. Hunger is just not something we have to put up with any longer in our culture.

Neither do we have to go around thirsty. Thirst is a desire that can be even more intense than hunger. When you are hungry, you can put off eating for hours and still function. Not so with thirst. If you are thirsty, really thirsty, you cannot think of anything else until the thirst is satisfied.

When Jesus said, "Blessed are those who hunger and thirst for righteousness," he was speaking to people who understood both hunger and thirst. In that culture, you were considered to be rich if you had food for tomorrow. Life-sustaining water had to be drawn from a well every morning. Hunger and thirst were constant, driving forces in the lives of Bible people. Their lives were directed toward obtaining food and water. Jesus uses the imagery of that constant driving need for food and drink to describe a driving desire for righteousness, a desire to do the will of God and to be in a fulfilling relationship with him.

Righteousness should have for us the same driving attraction as my grandmother's Sunday lunch. The sweet fragrance of relationship with him should call us to the table to be greeted by One who intensely wants to be with us. Deep-down and complete satisfaction is the promise for those who are hungry.

The Voice of God

Be still, and know that I am God.

PSALM 46:10

Moses heard it from a flaming bush. Young Samuel heard it as he was lying down one night to rest. In Jesus' day, a group of Greeks and Jews thought it was thunder. Jesus heard it in the midst of a crowd of mourners.

The voice of God has moved far more than the pens of prophets. He has spoken with life-changing power without need for pulpit or podium. As for myself, I have heard no thunderous rushing water, but I have been convicted by the honesty of a fourth-grader. I have not witnessed a descending dove, but I have seen Jesus smile over a glass of iced tea in a restaurant booth. I have been directed by neither cloud nor pillar of fire, but have known in my heart, "This is where I am supposed to be." I have not heard angelic voices in celestial praise or seen the heavenly armies standing ready, but my spirit has been nudged and urged and prodded.

In the silence of private pain, I have heard words that offered a lifeline for my soul: "My grace is sufficient for you. My grace is sufficient for you." The same silence has been broken by a startling call to action: "You have stayed on this mountain long enough. Now break camp and advance."

God, in his speaking, whether he uses a person or a circumstance, or comes straight to my heart, seems to require of me stillness, silence, vision. I cannot hear with moving lips, and I cannot see with downcast eyes. I cannot bask in relationship when busyness holds me in its grasp. I cannot understand his message when my finger is in the face of the messenger. Nor do I seem to be able on my own power to break free and to move from bustle to peace, from denial to honesty, from pointing to reflecting. The same voice that summons my action first calls me to quietness. The same Spirit who empowers also pulls me into relationship. The same Lord who sends me out invites me in to renew my covenant and to feast with him.

How can I hear if I won't be quiet? How can I see if I will not look? How can I learn if I will not be still?

Open my ears and silence my babbling. Close my eyes and focus my vision. Slow my pounding, hurried heart. Break the silence that only you can create, that I may hear your voice.

Laugh!

A happy heart makes the face cheerful.

PROVERBS 15:13

We laughed until tears rolled down our cheeks. I was team teaching in a fourth-grade class, which broke into a thunderous roar that we could not stop. Cathy, the classroom teacher, had made one of those slips of the tongue that we all fear will happen.

We were working on a practice test. Cathy was reading sentences, and the students were deciding whether or not corrections were needed. The sentence she was to read was: "The cat crept on the stairs." A little imagination will tell you what Cathy had said instead of "crept."

In her defense, I must say that Cathy has both a cat and a set of stairs at her house. She was only speaking from experience. The unexpected word slipped out, and an instant hush overtook the room. Cathy couldn't hold it back. As soon as she broke up, the whole place fell apart.

"I knew that was going to happen!" she said between cackles. She was laughing, the kids were hysterical, and I could hardly catch my breath because I was laughing so hard.

Recovery took awhile, but when it was all over, it seemed somehow that we all knew each other better. The students were reminded that teachers are human beings who make mistakes and have a sense of humor. Cathy and I were reminded that the time we have with our students is to be enjoyed. We were all refreshed and relaxed. During the rest of the day, I often saw Cathy drift away in thought, spread a smile across her face, and shake her head in disbelief.

The healing, cleansing power of laughter is not something newly discovered. Laughter has been written about, sung about, captured on film, and studied. Norman Cousins wrote about laughter in his book *Anatomy of an Illness.**
Cousins watched old movies and TV shows, and had laughed his way to recovery from a devastating illness. Bill Cosby, in his first interview following the death of his son, told Dan Rather and the nation, "It's time to tell the people that we have to laugh." He was simply suggesting healing through laughter.

Other than a career as a stand-up comedian, the teacher's profession probably allows for more laughter than any other. Kids are funny. They do and say funny things. Laugh with them. Laugh at yourself. We all make goofy mistakes. Why keep them to yourself? Kids of all ages enjoy seeing their teachers laugh. Laughter gives us entrance into the human race in their eyes and makes us approachable. It supersedes professional distance; it transcends all academic functioning levels.

Laughter creates a genuine person-to-person connection. You have a lot of important things to do today. Do them well, but don't miss out on the laughter.

*Norman Cousins, *Anatomy of an Illness: As Perceived by the Patient* (New York: Bantam, 1981).

# Dust Cloud of Rejection

Jesus answered, "If you want to be perfect, go, sell your possessions and give to the poor, and you will have treasure in heaven. Then come, follow me." When the young man heard this, he went away sad, because he had great wealth.

MATTHEW 19:21-22

I knew something was wrong as soon as I pulled into Sandy's driveway for Monday afternoon Bible study. Shari was sitting on the steps alone. The look on her face was one of defeat. I sat down beside her and put my arm around her fallen shoulders.

"It's Mike, isn't it?"

Silence.

"Can you talk about it?"

She spoke only with tears that dripped one by one onto her shoes. Her tears carried with them three years of compassionate frustration. Shari was a not-quite-tenured teacher who had an enthusiasm that I would like to bottle and give away at faculty meetings. She was young, single, and able to invest time and energy that many of us did not have. Mike became her student during her very first year of teaching. She took him under her wing that year, and he responded with a desire to be both sheltered and set free.

Shari made Mike a part of her extended family. She took him home with her for dinner and games with her parents and brothers. She took him to Sunday school and church on Sundays, enrolled him in church-league basketball, and took him to camps and youth rallies. She bought him as many hamburgers and French fries as a thirteen-year-old could eat, as well as his first pair of real leather basketball shoes for basketball season. He proudly wore a Kentucky Wildcats sweatshirt just like the one Shari had given her brother for Christmas.

In the midst of all of this, however, Mike would sometimes disappear for days on end. His mood would swing from hot anger to cold indifference at the drop of a hat. His notebooks were filled with gang graffiti. Whenever he was called in for disciplinary action at school, he stubbornly held his ground, especially when he perceived that he had been unjustly accused by a teacher. He often threatened to run away.

Such had been the case on this day, and Mike had ended up in the office with a discipline referral. On this day he was talking to no one, including Shari. She had driven him home in silence and had left him to be swallowed up by the neighborhood that beckoned him to be like everybody else. She had driven away in frustration and fear.

"What if I'm not doing enough? What if I lose him no matter what I do?"

Jesus offered eternal life to a rich young ruler, but it wasn't enough. The young man thought that his world could take care of his needs. Jesus could only watch him walk away. We may offer love and hope, but the truth is that sometimes our offer will be rejected. Jesus inhaled the dust cloud of rejection, and so will we. Jesus never stopped offering himself. Neither will we.

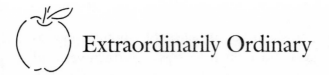 Extraordinarily Ordinary

Better is one day in your courts than a thousand elsewhere.

PSALM 84:10

It is an ordinary day. The sky is gray with clouds that promise no freshening rain. The earth is green but dull, without vibrant sun to brighten it. The air hangs heavy, with no cool breeze to awaken me. Today is not a holiday calling for celebration. No crisis begs for my time and attention. I am not moved by the magnificence of creation. The lawn needs mowing, and the flower garden needs to be weeded. I cannot allow myself to think about grass or weeds as I pull my car out of the driveway.

My car takes its usual place in the school parking lot. My "Needs Attention Now" file at school will be the first order of the day, promising to be empty by noon. I have the usual turkey sandwich and carrot sticks in my lunch bag. The coffee in the teachers' lounge is fresh and hot. Students file into my classroom, ready to begin their work. My assistant, Carol, is moving from desk to desk, answering questions. Routine prevails. Organization pays off. Planning works. It is an ordinary day.

This would be such an easy day to simply rely on my own strengths, an easy day to just coast through. I will be busy—I am always busy—but this day will not be any busier than any other. I could spend this day doing my job and, at day's end, pat myself on the back for having done it well.

I could forget on this ordinary day that, in the beginning, the God of the universe laid the cornerstone of the earth and set it spinning. I could forget that he gives orders to the morning and names to the stars, that nothing is hidden from him. I could choose not to rely on him today since my weaknesses are apparently not causing me to fall. I could choose to forget that every strength I have is a gift. I could forget that God can recite the number of my days as readily as the number of hairs on my head.

But I will not forget. I will not forget that God is sovereign over this ordinary day. At its end, I may count no miracles. The most extraordinary aspect of this day may be that it is so ordinary. The sun rose, the earth spins, I awoke again to go to work. The gifts God has given me as strengths are set in motion to do the work he has given me to do. I am able to have a day filled with routine but void of crisis—an extraordinarily ordinary day for which I am extraordinarily grateful.

The Class of '71

And he has given us this command: Whoever loves God must also love his brother.

1 JOHN 4:21

In 1981, I attended my ten-year high school reunion. I am not sure I would have gone had I not been paid to be there. (This was during my musician days, and my band was contracted to play for the dance that followed the usual dinner and festivities.) I was both a participant and an observer that night.

Nothing much had changed in ten years. The show-offs still showed off. The snobs still snooted and rooted together. The "regular" people visited with each other, and many went home after dinner. The same crowd from the class ahead of us who had crashed parties in high school crashed our reunion. The party crowd, including the crashers, partied until the wee hours of the morning, topping the night off with many of the partiers jumping, fully clothed, into the swimming pool. Like I said, nothing much had changed in ten years. I left the reunion well paid but empty; reintroduced, but not reunited.

Ten years later I decided not to attend my twenty-year reunion. It seemed to me that I held nothing in common with my high school classmates, and reconnecting with them was pointless.

Nothing in common? Pointless? I have since thought better of it. How could I think that I had nothing in common with three hundred-plus people who share with me the same birth year and for many the same birthplace? Perhaps we do not share the same goals and values in our adulthood, but our histories are forever united. We all shared Sunday nights with Ben Cartwright and the boys, and Monday nights with Marshall Dillon. We loved bell-bottoms and feared Vietnam. We all know where we were the day JFK was shot. We remember bomb shelters, Fizzies, Kent State, and Woodstock. We wore P.F. Fliers and Red Goose shoes, loop earrings and POW bracelets. We saw the rise of the Beatles and the fall of Elvis, the fall of the Beatles and the rise of Elvis. We were mothered by June Cleaver and amazed by Ward's ability to spare the rod and still discipline the child. We can identify mohair and Maynard G. Crebbs.

We were raised, as no generation before us, to fear annihilation, yet we roamed our neighborhoods on summer nights unattended and unafraid. We were offered no rose-colored glasses, yet we remember Norman Rockwell's America. We flew from our parents' nests, determined to change the world but not ourselves.

The world is changed and so are we; so am I. The members of the class of 1971 and I have gone in as many directions as we are in number. Yet the water under our bridges is tinted by the world that we shared together. I deeply value that world and those who remember it as well.

We are a unique volume of history, as is each class that walks the stage on a warm spring evening. Current graduates walk, as we did, into a world that invites them to change it and out of a story that is singularly theirs. May they, may we, never lose sight of its value.

# A Boulder Necklace

Things that cause people to sin are bound to come, but woe to that person through whom they come. It would be better for him to be thrown into the sea with a millstone tied around his neck than for him to cause one of these little ones to sin. So watch yourselves.

LUKE 17:1-3

The game was a display of baseball at its very worst. A swung-and-missed pitch resulted in a ground-pounding exhibition of temper. A called strike brought a "Have-you-lost-your-mind?" look at the umpire. Elbows and steel cleats dug into the anatomies of the players on the opposing team, followed by denials of anything intentional. Win or lose, someone on this team always spit in his hand just before the postgame handshaking ritual. The players on this offensive team had a role model: their coach.

If you stand near this team's dugout just before game time, you can often overhear the coach making slurs of various descriptions toward the opposing team's players and coaches. Waves of laughter roll through the dugout. After the game, if the opposing team wins, they got all the breaks and had the umpires in their pockets. If his team wins, they congratulate themselves not only for skill but for getting by with breaking rules and making their opponents look foolish. The youngsters, both individually and collectively, are a mirror of their coach.

Scripture speaks several times about the importance of not causing someone else to sin or to stumble. First Corinthians 10:28-32 tells us that eating food sacrificed to idols could be a stumbling block to others, so we need to be careful about that. Romans 14:13 tells us to make up our minds not to put any kind of stumbling block in our brother's way. That leaves the field wide open for us to decide about how our attitudes and behaviors might influence other believers.

But the words in Luke 17 are the ones I find most troubling and convicting for those of us who work with children and young people. Jesus puts a "woe" on those who cause "little ones" to sin. Woe is not a good thing. He does not go into great detail about the woe, but says that a person who causes a little one to sin would be better off if someone tied a heavy rock around his neck and threw him in the ocean. I always have to draw a deep breath after reading that verse. The point is that wearing a boulder necklace at the bottom of the ocean is a more pleasant circumstance than Jesus' "woe." To that I say "Whoa!" for I affect the lives of "little ones" every day.

Those of us who choose to teach professionally or coach voluntarily commit ourselves daily to influencing minds and bodies. Well-taught minds make the grade. Well-coached bodies win the game. But every mind-body combination comes equipped with a spirit, and therein lies our greatest responsibility. Our attitudes and the way we choose to treat other people are contagious. The team I observed on the baseball field was infected with their coach's win-at-all-cost attitude and his arrogant disregard for others. He had no idea that Jesus had a "woe" planned for him.

Let's draw a deep, cleansing breath as we face our day. Let's remember the necklace we might be asked to wear. Let's take our day seriously. Let's say "Whoa" before we face the "woe."

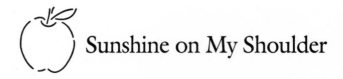 Sunshine on My Shoulder

Do nothing out of selfish ambition or vain conceit, but in humility consider others better than yourselves.

PHILIPPIANS 2:3

Sometimes you just do not get to do what you want to do. Comfort is a powerful persuader. One rainy morning, watery rhythms outside my window whispered suggestions to me to stay in bed. I turned over and allowed myself to fantasize the indulgence of a long morning nap followed by pillow-propped book reading, a steaming cup of coffee in hand. I was drifting along in the wonder of it all when the snooze alarm rattled me to reality. My feet found the floor with a great sense of responsibility and resolve. "Not today," I said to the call of comfort. "That scenario will have to wait for another day."

Any teacher knows that rainy days at school are usually excellent teaching days for everyone except the physical education teacher, who, of course, had an outdoor activity planned. Students tend to be a bit subdued by the rhythm of rain on the windows. On this day, in spite of my early morning struggle with mellowness, I found myself energized by my students' willingness to stay on task. At day's end, I was asking where the time had gone. This wet, gloomy day had not been just a "good day," it had been a very good day.

Rainy days always beg me to stay in bed, but sunshine calls me outdoors. I'm convinced of it. Why else would it peek through my classroom window on a brisk fall day? It wants me to come outside and play.

One sunny day resurrected the free spirit within me, beckoning me to take the afternoon off and go for a long bike ride in the country. I could fill my lungs with fresh air and empty my mind of unnecessary clutter. I was shaken to reality as the "squawk box" on the wall beckoned me with a different message:

"Mrs. Page, would you come to the office, please? You have a parent here to see you."

"I knew I should have taken the afternoon off," I thought as I made my way through the sunny courtyard to the main building. Standing in front of the office was a parent I had not seen since her daughter had left my class eight years before. With her was Elizabeth, her daughter and my student from so many years ago. Our reunion was warm and fun. Elizabeth had recently returned home after completing a job-training course. She just wanted to stop by to say hello and thanks. I was bursting with pride for all that she had accomplished. Thank you's are so unnecessary in the teaching profession, but they do feel so good.

On my way back to the classroom, I took in a chest-full of fresh fall air. Sunshine nudged my shoulder. "Not today," I said with renewed energy in my step, "I have important work to do."

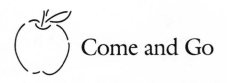

Come and Go

Come to me, all you who are weary and burdened, and I will give you rest.

MATTHEW 11:28 (NCV)

I read recently that the number-one reason Americans go to the doctor is fatigue. We are overworked, under-rested, and drained. Many of us in the teaching profession have jobs that are physically tiring. Many of us have reason to be physically exhausted at the end of the day.

For most of us, however, it is not physical fatigue that pulls the very life from us. Some have compared teaching fatigue to battle fatigue. We have to be constantly on our toes and alert. We are required to make as many as twelve hundred decisions a day, many of them in a split second. We are in demand every moment of our workday. We continuously hear our name spoken. Our work is constantly interrupted, often by trivia. We are sometimes expected to do our job with inadequate space and materials. No wonder we are exhausted physically, mentally, and spiritually.

In chapter 6 of Mark's Gospel, Jesus gathers with his disciples to talk about their teaching. Jesus had sent them out in pairs into the villages. They went out to teach with sandals on their feet and clothes on their backs. No sack lunch, no visual aides, and no bus fare. They walked from village to village, healing, casting out demons, and teaching. When they returned from their travels, they were exhausted. They couldn't wait to tell Jesus all that had happened, but so many people were gathering around that they couldn't even find time to eat, much less talk. Jesus made a profound suggestion. "Come with me by yourselves to a quiet place and get some rest" (Mk 6:31).

The key word here is "come." Jesus sent them out to teach and to labor, but when it was time to rest, he invited them to come with him. He wanted to renew their connection by spending time together. He was the source of their power to teach and heal, and he was their place of rest.

I can only imagine what it must have been like to climb into a boat and sail away with Jesus and a group of friends. I imagine that they told story after story as the wind pushed them across the water. Some probably slept while others talked Jesus' ear off. I imagine that some, maybe John, simply sat and enjoyed the quietness of Jesus' presence. I think maybe I would have joined him.

Jesus calls me away just as clearly as he called those twelve men that day. He understands the demands of my life, but he also knows the value of renewal. He calls me to sit by a mountain stream and enjoy his presence. He calls me to gather with other teachers, whose days have been as exhausting as mine, and share with him every care, heartache, and victory. He lures me to wrap myself in the warm covers of my bed on a Saturday morning and share a long cup of coffee and my every thought with him. He promises me the gift of rest. All I have to do is come.

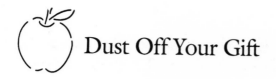

Dust Off Your Gift

Do not neglect your gift.

1 TIMOTHY 4:14

It's a good thing that there is no law against classroom neglect. I would have been handcuffed and hauled away to dust-bunny prison. This past year just sort of got away from me.

I admit I am a pile maker, not a file maker. I know what is in each pile and when it needs attention. No one else could make the least bit of sense of it, but I manage to finish whatever needs to be finished and to turn in what needs to be turned in, usually on time. I always intend to file things, but often it just does not get done. My piles are neat, by the way, but they tend to increase in size and number as the year goes by.

Necessary creature comforts fill shelves in my room that could be used otherwise. I have a microwave oven in the back of my classroom, which means a supply of microwave popcorn sits on one shelf. I admit to excess when it comes to coffee cups and tea bags. One never knows when another teacher might come in and ask for some refreshment, or when I might leave my cup somewhere and not have time to find it. I probably don't need all six of the cups that usually have taken up residence on my shelf by the middle of May. Neither is it necessary for me to have seven flavors of tea, since I always choose my one and only favorite.

Like every other teacher with more than five years' experience, I also have teaching materials that could stand to be thinned out. Dust-coated workbooks and masters wait patiently for someone to rediscover their worth.

Fortunately for me, the Lord gave me an assistant this year who is a file maker. She has spent the year organizing my materials in a way I could only dream of. The last two days of school, however, she tore into my classroom and my piles. We both admitted serious neglect. The dust was so thick in places, we could have planted a crop. Carol would hold something up and say, "What is this, and how long has it been since you used it?" Usually my answer resulted in a clunk into the wastebasket. Sometimes she would see a pained expression on my face.

"Does it have sentimental value?" she would ask.

"Maybe a little, but I'll get over it."

Carol was simply doing something she had been itching to do all year, using her God-given gift of organization. I had not only neglected my classroom. I had neglected to encourage her to freely use her gift. Had I released her completely to use her gifts all year, everyone would have benefited. And it's the same way when we free others. Life just works better that way. You should see my room now that Carol has had her way with it. I wonder what other persons I know have gifts waiting to be used.

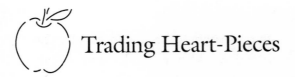

Trading Heart-Pieces

Let me inherit a double portion of your spirit.

2 KINGS 2:9

Freddie walked out of my classroom for the last time, report card in hand, and middle school in his future. I watched through the window as he swung on every awning pole along the sidewalk on the way to his grandmother's car. I had seen Freddie walk this same path in the same way, hundreds of times, but today was different. Two years of roller coaster emotion pushed hot tears down my face as I witnessed this scene one final time. I wondered, as I always do when students leave my care, what he would do with the piece of me that he carried away with him. And I thought about how I had been changed by the part of him that will be with me as long as I live.

My time with Freddie has caused me to examine myself as a professional, as a human being, and as an ambassador of God's love. Thanks to Freddie, I have learned to be less self-sufficient and more humble. Having to ask for help from administrators, other teachers, and assistants is not my usual style, but this time I had no choice. Some of those I went to strongly supported me, while others left me treading in deep water.

I have discovered that after nearly twenty years of teaching, I can still be manipulated by a ten year old. This was not a pleasant discovery, but it has moved me to find the value of tough love and the teaching power of natural consequences. I have learned anew the importance of not giving up, of going to plan B or C or Z if necessary. I have watched the power of consistency in response to continuous testing. Many times it seemed Freddie was thinking, "If I do this, or call her that, will she still be here tomorrow?" He has and I have. I have learned the truth of the "crisis breeds intimacy" theory.

Crisis has been no stranger to this relationship, and I have never cared more deeply for a student or his family. I have watched as one fearful of attachment found the courage to trust, taking baby steps forward. I have rejoiced as two little eyes finally met mine and stayed.

I stared out my window as Freddie and his grandmother drove away. Clutched in my hand was the tiny crystal cross he gave me to remember him. Sealed in my heart was a fragment of him that was uniquely mine. Deep within him was a part of me that could be given only to him.